ReDISCOVERING
the lost
KINGDOM

KINGDOM SECRETS TO RESTORING
NATIONS BACK TO GOD

VOLUME ONE

ABRAHAM JOHN

Rediscovering the Lost Kingdom
Copyright © 2018 by Abraham John

Maximum Impact Ministries
P.O. Box 631460
Littleton, CO 80163-1460

www.maximpact.org
email: mim@maximpact.org
(720) 420-9873

ISBN: 978-0-9972591-8-6

Printed in the United States of America

Contents

Preface

Whether you realize it yet or not, your heart has been searching for a lost kingdom. Until you find it, you will never really be happy on this earth. It doesn't matter who you are or how much wealth you possess, which religion you believe, or what type of church you attend; nothing will satisfy you or be an adequate substitute. You were created to live in a kingdom. Religion made us believe that we are looking to go to heaven.

God did not create mankind to live in heaven. Believe me, it is not in the Bible. Adam was not created to go to heaven and he did not lose heaven when he fell. If you die today you will go to heaven to wait, but when the time comes you will return to earth to rule and reign with Christ. Your purpose is always connected to planet Earth, in this life and in the next.

Humans have three basic physical needs: food, clothing, and shelter. Humans also have emotional and spiritual needs. If they are not all met, one will feel unfulfilled or as if something is out of place in their heart. God created man as a three-part being, consisting of spirit, soul, and body. He cares about each of these components and their needs.

Humans have six fundamental needs, and when they are met, their physical, emotional, and spiritual needs are all covered. People everywhere are working hard to meet these six needs.

They are:

A country or community where they are happy

Fulfilling relationships

Significance

A government that administers righteousness, justice, truth, and mercy

Safety

Pleasure

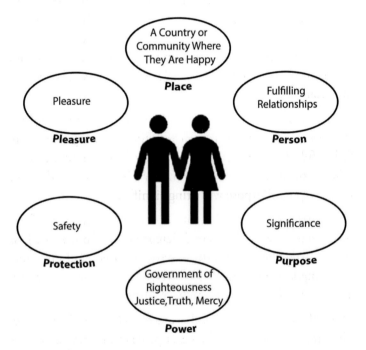

Everything we do in life is geared toward meeting one of the above-mentioned needs.

From a kingdom perspective, we are all looking for 6 Ps.

The first is a **P**lace: That place is the kingdom. People in developing nations interpret it as migrating to a developed country. People in developed countries think it is moving to a better part of town or to a bigger house. Once we move, we realize that places and things quickly lose significance.

The second is a **P**erson: We are created to have an intimate relationship with at least one other person. When we do not have that we will feel unfulfilled. We are created for companionship and connection. It begins with the relationship with our parents, then friends, then a life partner, coworkers, etc. In the kingdom, the most important relationship is with the King. Every other relationship we have is a reflection of our relationship with Him.

The third is **P**urpose: Without purpose life is meaningless. Whatever we do, if we are not fulfilling our purpose we will feel unfulfilled. Every person is looking for his or her purpose. When you discover the kingdom of God you will discover your purpose. Purpose will bring significance.

The fourth is **P**ower: Humans love power, but most of the time we misuse it. There are different kinds of power, such as money, influence, political, military, spiritual, and demonic. The kingdom of God is the source of all true power and authority. All authority flows from Him.

The fifth is **P**rotection: We all want to feel safe and protected. The kingdom of God is the safest place to be because there is no one greater or stronger than our King Jesus.

The sixth is **P**leasure: Since we lost the kingdom people everywhere are looking to be entertained or to have fun. It is the search of every human heart. Righteousness, peace and joy in the Holy Spirit compose the culture of the kingdom of God.

Throughout history, people in every culture have been looking to meet these six needs. No system, religion, or government has been able to meet these needs for us yet. People everywhere are disappointed and feeling unfulfilled. Man has not ended his search yet. People are born with an *instinct*, or *hunger*, that says there is a place and a person somewhere out there, and if they can discover it, all their abovementioned needs will be satisfied.

They keep trying new methods and places but come across the same fate as others before them and are left wounded and broken. Is there a solution to this dilemma? Is there a system, person, or place where they will be able to have all their needs met? I believe there is.

I believe that man's search for this place and person that fulfills all their needs will end only when they rediscover the kingdom of God, and Jesus Christ their King. We have been telling people that God, or Jesus, will fill the void in their lives. But I have seen people with Jesus in their lives still feeling empty and unfulfilled. We forget to tell them that Jesus is the *way* or the *door* to a place. We separated Him from His kingdom and offered just Jesus to the people. They only received part of the gospel; though they received Him they are still walking around empty and with unmet needs.

Once they discover Jesus *and* His kingdom, they will find the keys to fulfilling relationships and they will discover their purpose, which will give them significance and everything

8

else they need. The kingdom of God is a country whose culture is made of righteousness, peace, and joy. That is the real pleasure.

The kingdom of God has a government that administers righteousness, justice, truth, and mercy. When you are in the kingdom of God, you will know that it is the safest place to be and has an unlimited supply of resources, both natural and spiritual. This is where you will feel most secure and protected, regardless of where you are on the earth. You could be thrown into a lion's den and still be safe. God and His kingdom are everlasting and unshakable (Psalm 145:13; Hebrews 12:28).

Why do we say *rediscovering the lost kingdom*? Man was created and was living in the kingdom of God originally. We lost it because of our disobedience. God is merciful and decided to restore it to us. He knows that we can't function without it and will keep searching until we find it. Or we will try to substitute it with other things that are destructive.

That is why Jesus said, "Seek FIRST the kingdom of God and His righteousness, and all these things shall be added to you" (Matthew 6:33, emphasis added). When you discover God's kingdom, your search for the *place* will end. You can't discover His kingdom without meeting the King. When you meet Jesus, the King, your search for a *person* will end.

When you discover the kingdom, finally you will understand your *purpose*. When you fulfill your purpose, you will feel significant. You will understand the true *power* that God has made available for you in His kingdom. When you live in His kingdom you will feel His *protection* around you 24/7.

Nothing gives you more *pleasure* than knowing God and doing His will. Once you understand true joy, you will find out that all the other pleasure and fun you were having were just counterfeits.

This book is only an introduction to the journey of rediscovering that lost kingdom. I would encourage you to read it slowly and study it until it changes the way you think and function. At the end of this book you will find information on what to do next. I can guarantee this will be the most exciting and fulfilling journey you ever take in your lifetime. Many righteous men and kings desired to see what you see and read what you are about to read, but they did not get the opportunity (Matthew 13:17). In that sense, you are very special and privileged. Welcome to the journey of rediscovering the lost kingdom.

Chapter 1:
Kingdom 101

Chapter 1: Kingdom 101

"The Lord has established His throne in heaven,
and His kingdom rules over all."
Psalm 103:19

What is the Kingdom?

What was in the mind of God when He decided to create the earth and humans? Did He want to hear from heaven a bunch of people singing and playing music? Did He want to have a family and keep them separated from Him on a faraway planet? Or did He have something greater in mind? Our God is a King forever and ever (Psalm 10:16). He is not just a King; He is the King of all kings. He has a kingdom called the kingdom of heaven. When you think of heaven, try to think of it as a kingdom rather than a sky with clouds floating across it.

As I travel across the world and meet people from different nations, languages, and religions, I have discovered something very interesting. Every religion is made of the same basic ingredients. Whenever man came across something beyond his comprehension, he began to attribute it to a god. Whether it was water, rock, thunder, wind, the sun, anything and everything became a god to him. He began to worship the creation rather than worshiping the Creator.

They all have a story of creation (how the world came to be); they all believe in a god or many gods. They adhere to different types of rituals that are made of traditions and superstitions to appease that deity. They all believe in good and evil. And finally, they have a belief about what happens after they die, or about going to heaven. Thus various religions were formed.

Unfortunately, that religious spirit has crept into the church. It has deceived us all about our purpose and our mission on this earth. The purpose behind all of these religions, including Christianity, is the same which is to blind mankind from ever coming to the true knowledge of God and why He created them.

God's kingdom is everlasting and ever expanding. It is the nature of kings to expand their dominion and culture to new territories. For that, He decided to create a new planet called Earth. He wanted someone to take care of and manage that planet for Him. He created a species called humans, in His own image and likeness, to fulfill that task. **Mankind's job was and is to expand and establish the kingdom and the will of God on earth.**

As God's children we are supposed to be functioning just like Him. Knowing God is supposed to help us know more about ourselves because we are created in His image and likeness. We are supposed to be doing on earth what He does in heaven. Our responsibility is to get a glimpse of heaven and make it real on earth. In the beginning God created mankind and put them in a place called the garden of Eden. He knew that man needed a place called Eden to grow and become fruitful. **A kingdom is a territory or a nation ruled by a king.** If there is no territory, and no king, then there is no kingdom. Don't let anyone deceive you.

Compare this truth with your previous understanding of God's kingdom or the picture that comes to your mind when you hear the phrase *kingdom of God*. If that picture does not include a king and a territory He rules, then it is not a kingdom. It is pure religious deception.

A kingdom is made of twelve different components: 1) King, 2) Government/Ekklesia, 3) Family, 4) Culture, 5) Decrees & Laws, 6) Army, 7) Territory, 8) Education/Teachings, 9) Economy/Treasury, 10) Business/Industries, 11) Media, and 12) Agriculture. In the Bible, twelve is the number of divine government.

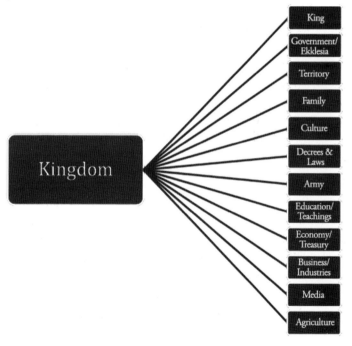

The difference between the kingdom of God and the kingdom of heaven is simple. The first reveals the *person* to whom the kingdom belongs and the second shows the *place* it is located, or where it is from. It is similar to saying the kingdom of

Nebuchadnezzar and the kingdom of Babylon, one shows ownership and the other shows location.

We are created in the image and likeness of God. *Image* stands for nature and creativity, and *likeness* represents similarity, behavior and capability. If you want to know about yourself, study and discover God. **You are created to act like God on the earth.** The more you know of God, the more you are supposed to know about yourself.

The Bible says no one has ever seen God (John 1:18; 1 Timothy 6:16). How do we know God, who is invisible? He chose to manifest Himself in many different ways. First, His attributes and glory are made manifest through the things He created (Romans 1:20). He chose to manifest His image and likeness through human beings (Genesis 1:26). He revealed His purpose and plan in His Word (Hebrews 1:1-2). Then, at last, He revealed Himself through His begotten Son, Jesus Christ (Colossians 1:15). So if someone wants to know God, he or she can know Him through creation, mankind, the Word of God, and by knowing Jesus Christ. When we put all of those revelations together, we will have an idea of who our Great God is.

God needs a specific place to dwell, so He created the heavens. Heaven is His throne. Everything God created requires a specific place and has a particular function. Fish need water; they were created to swim. Birds needs air; they were created to fly. And the stars need the sky; they were created to shine. Every creation is connected to a particular place. Where is the place for the mankind? Human beings need the garden of Eden (the kingdom of God), and their function is to rule and reign on earth (Genesis 1:26; Revelation 22:5).

When we hear the word *garden* we think of plants and trees with flowers and fruit. The garden of Eden was much more than a mere garden we see in our day and time. Though it might have had plants and trees, it was a *meeting place* for God and man and the *meeting point* between heaven and earth. It was the gate of heaven on earth. It was an atmosphere and environment created by God for both Him and man to function together in an intimate relationship. It was God's kingdom manifested in visible form.

The garden of Eden was the headquarters, or the command center, of the kingdom of heaven for the whole earth. God's will and plan for man was to make the entire earth just like Eden. Man's job was to duplicate what God showed and did in Eden. God's will was done in Eden as it was in heaven. If you could mess Eden up, you could mess up the entire plan of God for the earth. If you could take over Eden, you would get the entire planet. That is what happened with the fall of mankind. We lost the garden, and with that we lost the kingdom of God. With that we lost the rulership of the earth.

God created man to live in His kingdom. Ever since man lost the garden or the kingdom of God, we have been on a search for it throughout the centuries. You will read more about it in the next chapter. **It is impossible for mankind to live without a kingdom because we are created as kings**. There are two kingdoms operating on the earth right now. Every human being depends on one of those kingdoms; either the kingdom of God or the kingdom of darkness.

Man was created to extend and establish God's kingdom on earth. Genesis 1:26 is the purpose statement for man that was given by the Creator. Man was created to subdue and rule the earth and everything in it. If we do not understand Genesis chapters 1 and 2, we will not understand our purpose on earth—or the rest of the Bible.

Many are worried and concerned about the end times. They do not know the beginning well. The Bible ends where it began. If you want to know the end, look at the beginning. What I mean is this, Genesis 1 and 2 are God's original plan for man and earth. It was messed up, and ever since He has been restoring us back to our original intent. Revelation 21and 22 takes us back to the beginning once again. If we do not understand the beginning, we will not understand the present or the end.

We wasted many generations waiting for the end of the world or the rapture. We have been robbed and cheated by the devil through the religious spirit. As a result, we lost nations, our inheritance, family, governments—almost everything. It is time to restart from the very beginning. Let's shake off our religious masks and put on Christ.

Mankind was deceived by the enemy called Satan. Through deception, humans disobeyed God and sin and death entered them and the planet Earth. Sin is the operating system of the kingdom of darkness. It is a **S**atanic **I**nformation **N**etwork. Every thought or imagination that is in contradiction to God's Word comes from SIN. When sin entered humans, they lost the ability to think right and to see themselves as God sees them. Instead, they inherited a wrong view of themselves and God and were swayed from their purpose.

Man was created to live wholly dependent on God and His kingdom. The first temptation of Satan was to allure man to think and operate independently of God, which gave birth to humanism. Humanism is the tendency of mankind to trust and put themselves in the place of God.

Mankind looked for knowledge and enlightenment apart from God, tasting the fruit of the tree of the knowledge of good and evil. Know that there was some good in that tree in the beginning, but that good eventually turned into evil because God is not in it. There is some good in almost everything, but we need to look at the end and where it will ultimately lead us. If something does not lead us to life, then it is not worth pursuing.

After the fall, man and woman lost the glory of God and realized they were naked. They sewed fig leaves and covered their nakedness. They began to depend on their works in order to be accepted by God or to please Him. This gave birth to religion because sin distorts our view of God and His character.

After the fall of mankind, to accomplish His will on earth God chose a man called Abraham. Through his descendants, God established a nation called Israel. Israel became the manifestation of God's invisible kingdom on earth. Anyone who saw Israel knew they were special and different from all other nations. They were blessed above all others.

Israel was God's garden, or kingdom manifested. It was the gate of heaven, and God accomplished His will and plan on earth through them. But their glory did not last long, either. Because they disobeyed God, they were taken captive by other nations and lost the blessings and the land God gave them.

God created another *nation* for His counsel and purpose to be fulfilled. He decided to extend and share the blessing He bestowed upon Israel with this nation. To form this new nation, He chose a group of people from every existing nation and tongue on earth.

Because of the fall, man lost the rulership and dominion over the earth. Satan took hold of the opportunity and began to establish his kingdom and will on earth instead of God's. The earth is the Lord's property and He gave it to His children, but because of deception and the fall we lost dominion over the earth. Thankfully, God did not give up on us. He was committed to saving mankind and restoring them to their original intent. To accomplish that, He introduced a plan called salvation through His Son Jesus Christ. Adam was God's son (Luke 3:38), and once again He gives the authority to anyone who believes in Jesus Christ to become the children of God (John 1:12).

When Adam committed sin and fell, he lost seven things and it affected all of creation. Below are the seven things we lost:

Relationship with God and heaven

Provision and shelter (the garden of Eden)

Rulership and dominion over the earth

Glory of God

Kingdom of God

Purpose

All of creation came under the bondage of corruption

Once we are saved, we are supposed to go back to our original intent. If we do not, it means we have a wrong understanding about the salvation we received. Many are deceived by the religious spirit and think they are saved to go to heaven. Notice that *heaven, worship,* and *religion* are not included in the above list. Adam did not fall from heaven; he did not lose heaven when he fell. He lost the dominion and rulership of the earth. God decided to restore what we lost through the process of salvation. This is very important to understand.

God sent His Son Jesus Christ, who is called the Last Adam, to die for our sins and to save us from everything the fall and sin brought upon us. Once you are saved, you are supposed to be free from the consequences of the fall. Otherwise, the process of salvation is not yet complete.

Through salvation God restored to us everything we lost. Whoever believes in Jesus, God gave them the authority to become a child of God (John 1:12; 1 John 3:1).

Jesus said that if we seek His kingdom and righteousness first, then all the provision we need will be added to us (Matthew 6:33; Luke 12:30-31).

Everything Jesus did was to show us how to have dominion over the earth. Whether He walked on water, calmed the storm, gave a miraculous catch of fish, healed the sick, or cast out demons, He provided examples of how humans are supposed to live on earth.

Jesus gave us the same glory His Father gave to Him (John 17:22; 2 Corinthians 3:18).

Jesus came to give us the kingdom (Luke 12:32; 22:29).

The whole reason of salvation is to restore us back to our original purpose.

When the children of God are liberated, all of creation will be delivered from the bondage of corruption (Romans 8:19-21).

The Need for Another Garden

There arose the need for another garden, person, gate, or nation for God to operate through to govern His kingdom on earth. When man is restored to his original intent, he needs a command center or place of operation to establish God's kingdom and will on earth. This new garden is not called the garden of Eden like in Genesis. It is called *Ekklesia,* or the *Church.* The church is the garden of God through which He accomplishes His will and plan on earth right now.

When we are saved, at least some dimension of the life we (Adam – we were in him) once had in Eden should manifest in our lives. Adam did not have to sing for God to manifest in the garden. He had a Father-son relationship with God Almighty. That is the kind of relationship He always wanted with humans and it was broken for a while because of our disobedience (Exodus 4:22; Deuteronomy 32:18; 2 Samuel 7:12-16; 2 Corinthians 6:17-18).

That is why there was so much singing in the Old Testament: they did not know how to relate to God as their Father. That concept was too foreign for them. They needed singing to create a dwelling place for God. It is very sad today that many *saved* and *adopted* children still struggle to relate to God as their Father. It is hard for them to believe God dwells in them and they are His children.

Many are still seeking God's presence through singing, without knowing that He is living in them 24/7. They talk about going into His presence and coming out of it. They have been programmed by religion for so long that it is hard for them to think anything different. Their theology is still based on the Old Testament. Everything they do in their services is based on pre born-again concepts.

How did Jesus relate to His Father while He was on earth? How many songs did He sing each time before He could talk to Him? Show me one single reference from the New Testament and then I will believe your theology. We should learn to relate to God our Father as Adam did before the fall, and how Jesus did while He was on earth. That is His original design for us.

If you are having a hard time relating to God as your Father, I encourage you to become born again. It doesn't matter how long you have been in church. You may need some counseling to receive healing from the father wounds you might have from your earthly father, wounds that are hindering you from knowing your heavenly Father.

How many of you had to sing four songs before you had to talk or share with your earthly father, or for him to talk and share with you? Once we are saved, we enter into a Father-child relationship with God (Matthew 6:9; John 1:12). I could write a book on just that. **I define "salvation" as re-aligning with the original intent God has for the earth, for humankind, and restoring our relationship with Him as our Father and King.**

Jesus chose twelve men to establish this new nation (Matthew 21:43; 1 Peter 2:9). Twelve is the number of government in the Bible. He trained them and sent them out to preach the good news of the kingdom to the four corners of the earth. Everyone who received and believed the good news and the Lord Jesus Christ was added and became a part of forming this new nation. That nation is called the church or the *Ekklesia*. He decided to operate through the church to establish His will and kingdom on earth. Just like Adam and Israel, the church has not done a good job in fulfilling its assignment either. It is far from establishing His will and kingdom on earth. Instead, most are waiting to disappear from the earth.

The church is supposed to be the visible manifestation of the invisible kingdom. Those who see the church should understand and know how the kingdom of God operates. That was the case in Eden and the early church, and with the nation of Israel.

Becoming a Gate of Heaven

Each believer in Jesus Christ is a gate of heaven on earth right now. When you receive Christ, you become a dwelling place of God and a temple of the Holy Spirit. Now, please don't just seek His presence: seek Him. You have a direct connection with heaven. You have been chosen by God to release and execute His will and purpose.

The purpose of a gate is to give or deny access. When we become the gate of heaven on earth, we give access to God to accomplish His will on earth. In order to do that, we need to come into full alignment with God and heaven. Humans are the only species that has the legal right to allow or forbid anything on earth. That is the way God works in partnership with us.

In the Old Testament the gate of heaven was a physical place. When Jacob left his house to go to Padan Aram, his mother's place, on the way he reached a place called Luz and slept there. During the night he had a dream and God spoke to him in the dream. He saw a ladder that was set up between the earth and heaven, and the angels of God were ascending and descending on it.

When Jacob woke up he realized God was in that place and he called the name of the city Bethel, which means *the house of God.*

> "And he was afraid and said, 'How awesome *is* this place! This *is* none other than the house of God, and this *is* the gate of heaven!'" (Genesis 28:17).

In the New Testament it is not a building or a place that is called a house or gate of heaven, but a person.

> "Jesus answered and said to him, 'Because I said to you, "I saw you under the fig tree," do you believe? You will see greater things than these.' And He said to him, 'Most assuredly, I say to you, hereafter you shall see heaven open, and the angels of God ascending and descending upon the Son of Man'" (John 1:50-51).

To become a gate of heaven, a person needs to become a house of God. *House of God* means a place where God dwells. Where does God dwell now? Though He is in heaven, He dwells in each believer through His Spirit. We are called a house of God in the New Testament. He also dwells in His church. In the Old Testament the temple, or the house of God, was a building made of hands. In the New Testament the temple, or the house of God, is the people that receive God into their lives (John 2:19, 21; 1 Corinthians 3:16-17; 6:19).

Keep in mind that the church is not a building. The church is not a physical building made of bricks and iron. It is a building made of living stones, which are believers who are saved and washed by the blood of Jesus.

> "But if I am delayed, *I write* so that you may know how you ought to conduct yourself in the house of God, which is the church of the living God, the pillar and ground of the truth" (1 Timothy 3:15).

As a church, we are being built as the dwelling place for God. If we are the dwelling place of God, then we do not need to create another alternative or temporary dwelling for God through our singing. People say and do that because of the lack of understanding about New Testament theology and the doctrine of God.

> "In whom the whole building, being fitted together, grows into a holy temple in the Lord, in whom you also are being built together for a dwelling place of God in the Spirit" (Ephesians 2:21-22).

Why do we need to become the house of God or the gate of heaven? To release and execute God's kingdom purposes on earth and to identify and destroy the gates of hell and their works, as Jesus mentioned in Matthew 16:18.

The following diagram will help you understand the whole plan of God for us, and the church, in visual form.

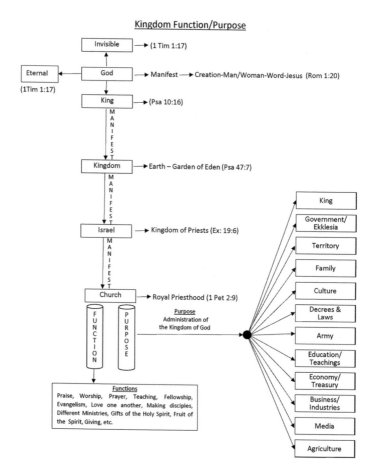

Kingdom Function/Purpose

Function and Purpose of the Church

We have been so focused on the *function* of the church that we are missing out on the *purpose*. We are so focused on how to live our lives that we are not fulfilling our personal purpose either. It's like the purpose of having a car or a house. The purpose of the car is to help us go from one place to the next. It functions because of an engine and many other parts working together to accomplish that purpose. If the car is not helping us to reach places, all its functions are wasted. A house is built to live in, not to decorate and install all the fixtures. If it is not used for people to live in then that house is not fulfilling its purpose, regardless of how beautiful it is and where it is located.

Jesus mentioned the purpose of the church in Matthew 16:18-19, "And I also say to you that you are Peter, and on this rock I will build My church, and the gates of Hades shall not prevail against it. And I will give you the keys of the kingdom of heaven, and whatever you bind (forbid) on earth will be bound (forbidden) in heaven, and whatever you loose (permit) on earth will be loosed (permitted) in heaven."

Any local church body that is not fulfilling the purpose mentioned above is wasting its time. It does not matter how well it may *function* as a body or how many members it might have. There are better programs in the world for fellowship, entertainment, and connecting with people, and usually better music and technology. This is not the purpose for which Jesus started His church. They are simply means to accomplish the purpose.

It is the same with individual humans. If we are not fulfilling the Genesis 1:26 mandate, it does not matter how much money we make, what kind of luxurious life we live, or which religious rituals we do. It is all rubbish at the end.

Chapter 2: Why is the Message of the Kingdom So Vital?

Chapter 2: Why Is the Message of the Kingdom So Vital?

> "I must preach the kingdom of God to the other cities also, because for this purpose I have been sent." Luke 4:43

Why is the message of the kingdom so vitally important to the body of Christ and the world? *Because Jesus' top priority is His kingdom.* He preached and taught about it more than any other subject. The entire Bible is about a King, His kingdom, and a royal family.

As you read in the previous chapter, we were created to live in Eden. Eden was the extension of God's kingdom on earth. God's will was done in Eden as it was in heaven. There is no sickness, poverty, curse, or death in heaven and there was no sickness, poverty, curse, or death in Eden. Adam was not created to die. He was an eternal spirit-being created in the image and likeness of God to administer His kingdom on earth.

God never mentioned anything about worship or going to heaven to Adam and Eve. They were created to live and reign on earth forever and ever. That is why the first and last chapters of the Bible say the same thing about the purpose of man (See Genesis 1:26 and Revelation 22:5.). We were created to reign on the earth.

The enemy deceived Adam and Eve. They fell from their position and from their relationship with God, and the whole creation came under bondage because of it. They did not fall from heaven; instead they fell from a position of governance and were cast out of Eden. Man lost the kingdom of God and began to live on earth without it. The enemy established a counterfeit kingdom (Babylonian System) and took man further away from God, luring him with things that satisfied his flesh, namely false power (control) and independence (false freedom).

We have been like kidnapped children, with our captor trying to pacify us and make us happy by giving us *toys* and everything else our flesh wanted. Outwardly we show we are happy, but in the spirit we feel unfulfilled and long to be back *home* with our *Daddy*. We all have been looking for our homeland.

The Gospel of the Kingdom

What is the gospel of the kingdom? "Gospel" simply means good news. The gospel of the kingdom means the good news of the kingdom. God did not give up on us. He wanted to reinstate us to our original position and restore His kingdom back to us. He knows that we cannot live fulfilled on earth without His kingdom. God sent His Son Jesus Christ with the message of the kingdom and its imminent return to earth. Since the time Adam lost it, our spirits have been yearning for our "homeland." Everyone on earth since Adam has been looking for a better place to live—for a better country and for a better government. We misinterpreted it and have been trying to sustain our spirits with luxury and fun.

In the Bible days, people longed to go to Egypt and live there because it was a prosperous and more developed nation than others at that time. Even Jacob sent his children there to buy food during famine. In our time, people from Third World countries long to immigrate to a developed country for better living and employment. People from the developed countries long to be at some vacation spot or resort. It's a universal thing for which every heart yearns.

All believers who have not yet discovered the kingdom of God, regardless of how long they have been saved and Spirit-filled, will sense there is something missing. They are longing for something just out of their reach, something more for them somewhere. Many interpret this feeling as a hunger for more of God or for His Spirit. Or to migrate to a more developed country or better community, but in truth their spirit is longing for the homeland they lost. Others misinterpret it as a longing for revival or the rapture.

Everyone who lived during the Old Testament time longed for a country too. Even though they were used by God and fulfilled their purpose, there was this longing in their spirit for a better country or city whose Maker and Builder was God (Hebrews 11:10). They were longing for the kingdom of God, which their forefather Adam lost. That is why the Bible says in Hebrews 11:13-16,

"These all died in faith, not having received the promises, but having seen them afar off were assured of them, embraced them and confessed that they were strangers and pilgrims on the earth. For those who say such things declare plainly that they seek a homeland. And truly if they had called to mind that country from which they had come out, they would have had opportunity to return. But now they desire a better, that is, a heavenly country. Therefore God is not ashamed to be called their God, for He has prepared a city for them."

These verses are powerful and reveal a hidden truth. Though I read this many times, I never understood what it really meant. It is extremely important to notice that these people in the Old Testament were *not* longing for more of God, more of His Spirit, or revival. They were all longing for a country, or as quoted above, a homeland. Notice the sentence, "If they had called to mind that *country* from which they had come out, they would have had opportunity to return." This refers to the heavenly country they came from, or which their forefather Adam came from. What country were they longing for? Why were they looking for a country and not for God? As I said earlier, we are created to live in God's kingdom. Until we discover it, we will not be satisfied.

They were all looking for a heavenly country, the kingdom of God, which was revealed in the New Testament with the coming of Jesus Christ. Heavenly country is another reference to the kingdom of heaven.

None of the Old Testament believers had the opportunity to hear the message of the kingdom, or the opportunity to live in it as we do today. That is why Jesus said in Matthew 13:17, "…for assuredly, I say to you that many prophets and righteous *men* desired to see what you see, and did not see *it,* and to hear what you hear, and did not hear *it.*" What is Jesus talking about? He is not talking about miracles, but seeing and hearing the message of the kingdom of God. There were plenty of miracles in the Old Testament times.

The time finally came when God decided to restore the kingdom to us. He sent His Son Jesus to reveal and teach us about it and show us how to live in it. That is why Jesus preached the kingdom of God more than any other subject. It was the first and last message He preached.

> "Now after John was put in prison, Jesus came to Galilee, preaching the gospel of the kingdom of God, and saying, 'The time is fulfilled, and the kingdom of God is at hand. Repent, and believe in the gospel'" (Mark 1:14-15).

Jesus was saying that the time is fulfilled for the kingdom of God to be restored to man. Jesus came to announce the imminent arrival of the kingdom of God to the earth. That is why He said, "The kingdom is at hand." "At hand" means near.

The reason the phrase *kingdom of heaven* appears only in the gospel of Matthew is because it is the first book of the New Testament and it is announcing the reentry of this heavenly country to planet Earth (Matthew 4:17; Mark 1:14-15). **Jesus came with a kingdom, or a country; His pivotal message was not taking us to heaven but bringing heaven to us.**

That is why He said in Luke 12:32,

> "Do not fear, little flock, for it is your Father's good
> pleasure to give you the kingdom."

He did not come to give us a church or a particular
denomination, but the very kingdom (Luke 22:29).

That is why Jesus began His preaching by announcing,
"Repent, for the kingdom of heaven is at hand" (Matthew
4:17b). What He meant by it is this, the country that all the
people on earth, especially the Old Testament saints, were
longing to see and live in is at hand. It's almost here. Wow!
What good news! The gospel is called good news and sadly we
have turned it into a religion.

In the New Testament we read that believers were longing for
a better city, not a country. We received the country already
through Jesus, but not the city yet. Which city are we seeking?
The New Jerusalem, which will come down from heaven, the
capital city of the kingdom of God on earth is what we should
be longing for as well.

> "But now they desire a better, that is, a heavenly
> *country*. Therefore God is not ashamed to be called
> their God, for He has prepared a city for them"
> (Hebrews 11:16).

> "For here we have no continuing city, but we seek the
> one to come" (Hebrews 13:14).

The Jews wrote the above verses. They were living (or had
lived) in Israel at some point and had been to the natural city
of Jerusalem. But the above verses say they were still longing
for another city that was yet to come. Which city are they

talking about? Most Christians from around the world desire to visit Israel and the city of Jerusalem, but the people who were living in Jerusalem were longing to be in some other city. Isn't that ironic? They were not longing for the natural city of Jerusalem but the heavenly one, the New Jerusalem.

> "He who overcomes, I will make him a pillar in the temple of My God, and he shall go out no more. I will write on him the name of My God and the name of the **city** of My God, the New Jerusalem, which comes down out of heaven from My God. And *I will write on him* My new name" (Revelation 3:12).

> "Then I, John, saw the holy city, New Jerusalem, coming down out of heaven from God, prepared as a bride adorned for her husband" (Revelation 21:2).

In the secular world, people define this longing for an imaginary country called utopia: a land that is beautiful and plentiful, where there is no sorrow or worry. If you are a human, you are born with that instinct. That search will only end when someone comes to Christ and discovers the kingdom of God. We have been preaching wrongly all these years. We told people only Jesus can fill the gap and longing in person's soul. That is not complete. People who have Jesus are still longing for something more. It's not a person they are looking for, but a country. Only the kingdom of God can fill that gap in us.

Many believers wait all their lives to die and go to heaven because they interpret the longing in their heart as a desire to go to heaven. Instead of discovering God's kingdom here on earth and fulfilling His purpose here, they waste a lifetime just waiting. The religious gospel has trained us to think that once you are saved your next stop is heaven.

> "The law and the prophets *were* until John. Since that time the kingdom of God has been preached, and everyone is pressing into it" (John 16:16).

This verse says that since the time of John the Baptist, the kingdom of God has been preached and everyone is pressing into it. Why is everyone pressing in to get in the kingdom of God? Why, when we preach our religious gospel of going to heaven, do only a handful get saved? It is because man is looking for a lost kingdom. When their spirit hears the announcement of the kingdom of God, they will run to get into it.

> Jesus said, "Verily I say unto you, that there be some of them that stand here, which shall not taste of death, till they have seen the kingdom of God come with power" (Mark 9:1 KJV).

What was Jesus talking about? If He was referring to His second coming, it would not be true. There is no way some people who were alive then would remain alive until His second coming. That would be impossible because a man does not live that long. He was talking about the day of Pentecost, when the Holy Spirit came with power. Since that day the kingdom of God began to operate on earth once again. That is what He meant when He said, "The kingdom of heaven is at hand." Many who had heard Jesus were alive to see it with their own eyes.

Nowhere in the book of Acts do we see any of the apostles preaching the kingdom-at-hand message. With the coming of the Holy Spirit in Acts 2, the kingdom of God arrived on earth and it has been operating here ever since. Does everyone see and experience it? No. Why? Because it does not come with observation, but a born-again believer can see it with his or her spiritual eyes. That is why Jesus said, "Most assuredly, I say to you, unless one is born again, he cannot *see* the kingdom of God" (John 3:3). The first result of the born-again experience is the ability to see the kingdom of God with the eyes of our spirit.

He also said in Matthew 12:28,

> "But if I cast out demons by the Spirit of God, surely the kingdom of God has come upon you."

The Holy Spirit comes with the kingdom of God. He comes to make it real to us and manifest it in the natural. That means that wherever the activities of the Holy Spirit are manifest, the kingdom of God is there. At present, without the Holy Spirit, no operation of the kingdom of God will ever be made manifest. It also does not mean that we only cast out demons by the Holy Spirit. Most people limit and know Him only for His gifts. He is much bigger than that. Do a study on the work of the Holy Spirit from Genesis to Revelation. He does everything God Himself does, because He is God. When a person or a place becomes fully yielded to the Spirit of God, the kingdom of God will manifest and be in full operation there.

When you discover the kingdom of God, the longing of your spirit will cease; for the very first time you will feel in your spirit that you are finally *home*. Until you discover it, nothing else will satisfy you, no matter how rich or poor you are or how long you have been Spirit-filled or in ministry. Instead of first seeking God's kingdom, which Jesus told us to do, believers today keep going from one revival meeting to another and from one conference to the next, being robbed and taken advantage of by so-called ministers. We must seek His kingdom with everything we have until we discover it. In Hebrews 12:28, the author concludes by saying,

> "Therefore, since we are receiving a kingdom which cannot be shaken, let us have grace…"

Many go after the teaching of grace these days too. The trouble is that before we can gain it we must first have a revelation of the kingdom of God. The above verse says we will have grace *after* we receive a kingdom that cannot be shaken, because grace is the operating system of the kingdom of God. In His kingdom, God deals with us through His grace. In computer terms, the kingdom is the *hardware* and grace is the *software*. What good is having the most powerful software in the world with no hardware to operate it? How does that benefit anyone?

Every nation has a political or governing system. India is democratic and China is communist in its government. The kingdom of God is a nation ruled by a King, who is God, and He uses grace as His governing system. Before we go after grace we need to discover His kingdom. That is why Jesus commanded, "Seek *first* the kingdom…" (Matthew 6:33).

Though the kingdom of God is now in operation on earth, not everyone will find it because it is like a treasure hidden in a field. Treasure is not easy to find, and only those who are very serious and willing to risk their life will find it.

> "Again, the kingdom of heaven is like treasure hidden in a field, which a man found and hid; and for joy over it he goes and sells all that he has and buys that field" (Matthew 13:44).

In the above parable, the *field* is the world and the *treasure* is the kingdom of heaven. It is hidden and God wants us to seek it. In another parable, Jesus compared the kingdom of heaven to a pearl of great price.

> "Again, the kingdom of heaven is like a merchant seeking beautiful pearls, who, when he had found one pearl of great price, went and sold all that he had and bought it" (Matthew 13:45-46).

What is God's Kingdom?

It is *very important* for you to know what the kingdom of God is before you start seeking it. Many people have fragmented ideas about the kingdom. A simple definition of a kingdom is a territory or a nation ruled by a king, where the king's will and plans are executed without any question. In this case, God is the King. He has a country called heaven and He wants to see His rule, or dominion, come to the earth.

Many think of the kingdom of God futuristically, something that will take place later in time or as a place or state they reach after they die. But the entire Bible is about a King, His kingdom, and His royal family. He decided to extend that kingdom to a planet called Earth. To manage that kingdom, He created a unique species in His image and likeness called human beings. That is our purpose: to represent God and manage His kingdom on earth.

The first mandate that was given by the King to man was to have dominion over the earth and everything He created in it (Genesis 1:26). According to the law of first mention, when God speaks about something for the first time, He reveals His heart and purpose concerning that thing. A mandate is an authorization to act, a charge to get things done, a commission to carry out an injunction, a precept to which to adhere, a guideline to follow without deviation, and an important order that must be obeyed. God gave the mandate to Adam and Eve. They were to have dominion over the earth and subdue and rule everything God created. But Adam failed in his assignment.

Man was deceived by the enemy and lost his dominion over the earth. Still, God did not change His purpose concerning man or His kingdom. He chose individuals and then a nation—the nation of Israel—to represent Him and His kingdom on earth. Eventually, they also rebelled and failed in their assignment. So Jesus said,

> "Therefore I say to you, the kingdom of God will be taken from you (Israel), and given to a nation (the church) bearing the fruits of it" (Matthew 21:43).

In the above verse, Jesus is saying the kingdom of God will be taken from the people of Israel and given to a nation. Which nation is He talking about? He is talking about the church. The church is a holy nation in itself, a nation within the nation you are living in (1 Peter 2:9). God sent His Son to die for our sins and to reinstate His kingdom purpose. He instituted the church, comprised of both Jews and Gentiles, to represent Him and His kingdom. This is not a new revelation I just discovered or made up. The revelation of God's kingdom is as old as the heavens and the earth.

Throughout the centuries the church has been asking God for particular benefits and specializing in a few aspects of the kingdom, instead of crying out for His kingdom to come. As a result, He sent the Salvation Movement, Healing Movement, Holiness Movement, Word of Faith Movement, and others. They are all different aspects of His kingdom, but not *the* kingdom. The time has come for us to receive the whole kingdom and administer it so that God's will is done on the earth *as it is in heaven.*

God's children need the same environment, like Eden, to survive. We won't go back into a physical Eden; instead He put Eden (the kingdom) inside of us (Luke 17:20-21). When God created man and put him on earth, He established a process, or a political system, to take care of man. That system is called the kingdom of God, which is the same system He has in heaven.

You can be saved and still not live in God's kingdom. According to Jesus, before we do anything spiritual or Christian, He wants us to seek His kingdom *first.* Now the question is, what is God's kingdom and how do we seek it? Since a kingdom is a country ruled by a king, as already mentioned, the word *kingdom* refers to the dominion of a king. Jesus is a King and He has a kingdom. His children are supposed to live in His kingdom. We are supposed to be seeking His dominion, or rule, in each area of our life. When an aspect of our life comes under the dominion or rule of Jesus, His kingdom has come and His will is done in that area of our life as it is in heaven. That is what He taught us to pray. Once our life comes under His dominion, then we can bring the same to the community we are living in, and eventually, to the whole nation.

When many people think of God's kingdom, they think it is all about power. Every kingdom has power but that is not all a kingdom has. Some say it is righteousness, peace, and joy in the Holy Spirit. That is the culture of the kingdom. That's the culture we are supposed to be living in. Compare that culture with the culture you are living in right now and notice the things people do to be happy, to have fun, and to have peace of mind!

The kingdom of God has an economy. We are supposed to live our lives based on kingdom economy, not the world's notions about money and success. Kingdom education is also different from the education system of the world. The world's education is focused on getting a degree and a job. Kingdom education is focused on discovering your purpose and developing your gifts and skills. A company can fire you from your job, but they cannot fire you from your purpose. An employer can remove you from your position, but he or she cannot take away your gifts and the skills you've developed.

Every person has at least one natural and spiritual gift. If we look at the lives of the disciples of Jesus, they were fishermen (or businessmen) before Jesus called them. That was their natural gift. After He called them, He gave them power and authority to heal the sick and cast out demons. That was their spiritual gift. Then He sent them out to do what He taught them to do. He said the worker is worthy of his food (Matthew 10:10b).

The kingdom has a health care system too. Do you know how many trillions of dollars our nation spends on health care? When kingdom health care comes, people live a healthy lifestyle. That healthy lifestyle protects their bodies from injury and builds their immune systems to fight disease and sickness. When you live in God's kingdom, He will show you what is good and not good for you to eat (Isaiah 55:2). There is no sickness in God's kingdom. The kingdom of God also has an agricultural system. We are not supposed to be eating what the world is producing, which is mostly poisonous and causes disease. The kingdom is supposed to have its own food production system.

Misunderstandings About the Kingdom

When Jesus preached the kingdom of God, He met the physical needs of the people first. He healed their sickness and promised them that if they sought His kingdom first, their food, clothing, and the basic things of life would be provided. For many years I thought there was no food or drink in the kingdom of God because God's kingdom is *spiritual.*

Many think that healing the sick and doing miracles is the kingdom of God. They are not the kingdom but just signs of the kingdom. When you go to a place or a location you will see the *signs* long before you reach your destination. Those signs lead you or tell you about the place you want to go. Jesus sent His disciples to heal the sick, to cleanse the lepers and to raise the dead, then tell them that the kingdom of God is near, or at hand. That means those miracles were not the kingdom but the signs that it was about to arrive (Matthew 10:7-8; Luke 10:9).

Jesus said: "My kingdom is not of this world" (John 18:36a). I thought there couldn't be anything material in His kingdom because it is not of this world, but that is not what Jesus meant. He meant that His kingdom is not *like* the kingdoms of this world because it is not from here.

In the kingdoms of this world, rulers abuse and oppress the citizens, and the king's servants fight for the king to protect him. They tax people to pay for what the king needs. Initially, they will promise them good things, but eventually they will rob and kill them. Jesus was saying, "My kingdom is not like that. I don't tax people to pay for My needs. My kingdom is self-sufficient and feeds the whole world. In My kingdom, I fight to protect the people. I didn't come to be served, but to serve, and to give My life as a ransom for many."

Many people quote the verse from Romans 14:17 that says the kingdom of God isn't about eating and drinking but righteousness, peace, and joy in the Holy Spirit. I once thought that there was nothing to eat in the kingdom of God and that we will fast every day if we are in God's kingdom.

That is far from the truth! In fact, Jesus said, "But I say to you, I will not drink of this fruit of the vine from now on *until that day when I drink it new with you in My Father's kingdom*" (Matthew 26:29). Jesus ate and drank with the disciples after His resurrection (Acts 10:40-41).

There is definitely food and drink in God's kingdom. What Romans 14:17 is saying is the kingdom of God is not *made* of food and drink; it most certainly *has* food and drink. In any kingdom, people have to eat in order to live. In fact, the first thing Jesus promised we would find when we discover the kingdom is food and other material things we need (Matthew 6:33).

Seeking God's kingdom does not mean getting baptized, reading the Bible, praying every day, sharing the gospel, or becoming a member of a church and speaking in tongues. The devil doesn't want you to discover God's kingdom. He wants to keep you a slave in his kingdom and to the system of this world till you die.

Some others, when they hear about the kingdom, think about going to church. Church is not the kingdom, but *the church* is its governing body. Because of confusion and misunderstanding of the kingdom of God, we have been misinformed about the truth of the kingdom message Jesus and the apostles preached.

The Kingdom Is Inside You

> "Now when He was asked by the Pharisees when the kingdom of God would come, He answered them and said, 'The kingdom of God does not come with observation; nor will they say, "See here!" or "See there!" For indeed, the kingdom of God is within you'" (Luke 17:20-21).

The kingdom of God is an invisible kingdom. We cannot see how it operates with our natural eyes (Mark 4:26-29). **God put His kingdom inside of us and it manifests to the world through the work we do.** It is God's desire that His will is done *on this earth as it is in heaven*. This can only be done through human beings because the earth was given to us. The new era of the kingdom of God began to operate with the coming of the Holy Spirit on the day of Pentecost. The *Ekklesia* of Jesus' kingdom began to operate from that day onward.

The kingdom of God belongs to God and He wants to give it to His children. Jesus said, "Do not fear, little flock, for it is your Father's good pleasure to give you the kingdom" (Luke 12:32). God wants His children to dwell in His kingdom. God gave the authority to become a child of God to those who believe in Jesus and receive forgiveness of sins. The church's primary purpose is to see God's will accomplished on earth as it is in heaven.

It will require an enormous amount of wisdom, power, and resources to see God's will accomplished on earth as it is in heaven. Everywhere I go I hear believers say they wish they had more money to help the kingdom, to start schools, to help ministries and churches, etc. They have a vision from God but lack the resources to fulfill it. The reason they say such things is because of a lack of understanding.

God never intended for us to depend on our limited resources, jobs, wisdom, and power to establish His kingdom on earth. It would not be justice on God's part to ask us to do something of which we are not capable. He knows we are limited without Him, and the resources we have are also limited. That is why He put the *unlimited* kingdom inside of us. Everything His kingdom has is unlimited. His wisdom, power, wealth, and resources have no limit.

Every time we see a need, instead of looking at the limited resources we have, He wants us to learn to tap into His unlimited resources and release it to meet that need: releasing heaven's resources to meet earthly needs. This is the way each child of God is supposed to operate. That is why Jesus told us to seek His kingdom first, and that all things are possible to those who believe (Mark 9:23). Believe what? Believe that the kingdom of God is inside of us and the King has made available all His unlimited resources to see His will done on earth as it is in heaven.

Right now, the Holy Spirit wants you to take off every limit that you (or others) have put on yourself. From the time we are born we are brought up hearing statements like, "You can't have that," "You can't buy that," "That's too expensive," "That's not for now," "You are stupid," and "You can't do anything right." The kingdom of darkness has programmed our minds with lies. We need to tear down those strongholds and replace them with a kingdom mindset. God speaks truth into us, truth we desperately need to believe and act upon.

Jesus told His disciples in Matthew 7:21-23,

> "Not everyone who says to Me, 'Lord, Lord,' shall enter the kingdom of heaven, but he who does the will of My Father in heaven. Many will say to Me in that day, 'Lord, Lord, have we not prophesied in Your name, cast out demons in Your name, and done many wonders in Your name?' And then I will declare to them, 'I never knew you; depart from Me, you who practice lawlessness!'"

We have been taught that the kingdom of God is all about healing, prophesying, and casting out demons. In the above verses Jesus is saying that you can do all those things and still miss the will of God for your life and the kingdom of God.

That astounds me! If casting out demons and healing the sick, prophesying, and doing many wonders are not His will, then what is the will of our heavenly Father? We live in a world where many believers run after miracles and prophetic words.

Don't misunderstand me. I am not against miracles, healing, prophesying, or wonders. They have their place in the kingdom. Most of the healings that take place today are for the believers in the church, but they are supposed to be signs for the unbelievers and we are supposed to be living in divine health. You may ask then, what is God's will? He revealed that in the prayer He taught His disciples: for His kingdom to come and His will to be done on earth as it is in heaven. In order to enter God's kingdom, we need to discover God's will for our lives. Sadly, many people these days run after miracles instead. There are many prophetic and healing schools that teach you how to prophesy and pray for the sick, but not very many schools help you discover God's will for your life and teach you how to live in His kingdom.

God's will for my life is not the same as His will for yours. Each of us is equipped to do something different.

> "Therefore, brethren, be even more diligent to make your call and election sure, for if you do these things you will never stumble; for so an entrance will be supplied to you abundantly into the everlasting kingdom of our Lord and Savior Jesus Christ" (2 Peter 1:10-11).

The above Scripture says we need to make our calling and election sure. When we do this, we will never stumble. When we are sure of exactly what we are called to do (God's will), an entrance will be supplied to the everlasting kingdom of our Lord and Savior Jesus Christ.

Once you seek God's kingdom and discover your purpose, it is still not easy to *enter* His kingdom. The enemy will fight and do his best to keep you in his fold. As long as you are a good church-going Christian you are not any threat to his kingdom; but the moment you try to renounce the kingdom of this world and enter God's kingdom, all hell will break loose. We are in the midst of an age-old fight between two kingdoms: the kingdom of God and the kingdom of darkness. They both want human souls.

> "And when they had preached the gospel to that city and made many disciples, they returned to Lystra, Iconium, and Antioch, strengthening the souls of the disciples, exhorting *them* to continue in the faith, and *saying,* 'We must through many tribulations enter the kingdom of God'" (Acts 14:21-22).

Chapter 3: Seek the Kingdom First

Chapter 3: Seek the Kingdom First

"But seek first the kingdom of God and His righteousness, and all these things shall be added to you." Matthew 6:33

J esus told us to seek His kingdom first, not revival. People are seeking all kinds of things: relationships, money, jobs, miracles, material things, success, fame—but nothing will satisfy them. Only the Creator knows the needs of His creation. When the Creator created us, He designed us in a way that we cannot live without a kingdom.

How would you feel if someone said, "From today on, I will provide the food, shelter, and clothing for you and your family so that you can be free to do what you were born to do"? That is exactly what Jesus is saying by telling us to seek His kingdom first. Then all the things we need in life will be added to us.

Jesus told us to seek His kingdom to free us. Many people do not feel free to do what they are born to do. They are stuck at a job they don't enjoy, but they are doing it to provide for their family.

Why did Jesus Tell Us to Seek His Kingdom *First?*

Man is designed and created to live in and build a kingdom

Without a kingdom, either the kingdom of God or the kingdom of darkness, we will not survive on this earth. We have a choice. It's up to us to live and build God's kingdom. If we do not do that, we will build up the kingdom of darkness or our own little kingdoms instead.

In every man is the desire to design, govern, rule, build, establish, raise up, and accomplish something, or to help someone else do it. When a man cannot do that, he gets frustrated. And if something doesn't happen the way he planned while he is doing that, he wants to destroy it. If a man does not have that desire in him, something happened to his manhood and it needs to be restored. A woman is designed and created to help a man build a kingdom, to be the queen by his side. If a woman does not have that desire, then something happened to her womanhood and it needs to be restored. It is their natural instinct.

In the gospel of Luke, we read that when the kingdom of God was preached, everyone pressed in to be a part of it. It was like they all had been waiting for something but did not realize what it was they were waiting for, until they heard the message of the kingdom. When they heard it, they recognized it and they ran to get inside.

> "The law and the prophets *were* until John. Since that time the kingdom of God has been preached, and everyone is pressing into it" (Luke 16:16).

Another verse says,

"And from the days of John the Baptist until now the kingdom of heaven suffers violence, and the violent take it by force" (Matthew 11:12).

When the kingdom of God is being preached, the natural response of man should be, "Yes, I want it!" You do not have to coerce or manipulate people. Just preach the kingdom of God and they will come.

Man is worried about his basic needs

The majority of people spend most of their lives working a job to provide food, clothing, and shelter for themselves and their families. Naturally, people are worried about what they are going to eat and wear, and where they are going to live. Jesus is saying that's not the way life in His kingdom ought to be, or how His children are supposed to live. He is saying that food, clothing, and shelter will be added to His children as a result of them seeking His kingdom. In His kingdom, the King provides for His children so they can spend their precious time here doing what is really important, which is discovering and doing His will.

The precious and short time we have on earth is not to be wasted trying to make a living. Life is more important than finding food, clothing, and shelter. For many people, the most precious asset they have is their house, which will perish after a while. We are supposed to be working for what is eternal: His kingdom.

When we seek His kingdom, Jesus will provide our basic needs, which would free us up to spend all of our time doing what He created us to do. When all the people on earth discover His kingdom, there won't be any hunger problem.

Jesus knows the side effects of worry and stress

Worry and stress are the root causes of many of the illnesses and diseases of the modern day. That is why He said repeatedly not to worry about our life but to seek His kingdom first. As our Creator, He knows what worry does to the body and mind.

Man is searching for a lost country

As I mentioned earlier, everyone on earth is looking for a better place to live and be happy. The human heart longs for the kingdom lost with the fall of Adam. The kingdom of God is the only country that will fulfill that longing. That is why He told us to seek His kingdom first.

Man is longing for a government

Every human is looking for a government to solve their problems, to provide for, protect, and take care of them. Since we lost the kingdom of God, man has come up with different forms of government and none of them has worked yet to solve our problems. We get tired of the unfulfilled promises our politicians make, and we elect a new government every few years.

We know in our heart that there is a perfect form of government somewhere out there that will work. There is only one perfect government that will fulfill the needs of mankind and that is the government of God. That is why Scripture states that the government shall be upon His shoulders (Isaiah 9:6), referring to Jesus. He came to this earth with a government and told us to seek it first.

Social and racial problems will be solved

All over the world, the church is infected and challenged by racism and the caste system because people do not live the reality of their salvation in their daily life. There is only one thing that will solve that problem and that is the teaching of the kingdom of God. When you were naturally born you became the citizen of your country, which thrives on racial prejudices and cultural pride.

Once you are born again, you become a citizen of God's kingdom. You no longer live based on your natural identity but based on your spiritual birth. Every born-again believer, from every nation and language, is a citizen of the same kingdom. There is no racial preference or discrimination in the kingdom of God. That is why Jesus told us to seek it *first.*

It is the priority of Jesus

God's priority is to see His kingdom established on earth, not to see all of us in heaven. Everything Jesus taught and preached focused on that priority. He began His ministry saying, "Repent, for the kingdom of heaven is at hand." There are many people who preach repentance these days, but they do not tell the whole story. They tell people they need to repent to go to heaven. That is not what Jesus preached. We need to repent because His kingdom has come. "At hand" means it is here. He sent His disciples to heal the sick, raise the dead, cleanse the lepers, and tell them the kingdom of God had come (Matthew 10:7-8; Luke 10:2-9).

There are many people that go around and preach and teach healing, and some people get healed but they remain hungry and broke. Jesus never preached or taught about healing. He preached the kingdom and healed the sick. He told us to do the same.

> "He sent them to preach the kingdom of God and to heal the sick" (Luke 9:2).

When Nicodemus came to Jesus by night to greet Him, He told him about the kingdom of God (John 3:3). He told another man to follow Him and when the man asked Him to let him go and bury his father first, He replied,

> "Let the dead bury their own dead, but you go and preach the kingdom of God" (Luke 9:60).

Jesus said this was His purpose for coming to the earth. "But He said to them, 'I must preach the kingdom of God to the other cities also, because for this purpose I have been sent'" (Luke 4:43).

People everywhere are worried about the end times. They want to know when the world is going to end. The disciples of Jesus had the same concern, and they asked Jesus to tell them how to know when the end would come. Jesus gave them (us) a very specific answer to know when the end will come, which we have been ignoring for way too long.

> "And this gospel of the kingdom will be preached in all the world as a witness to all the nations, and then the end will come" (Matthew 24:14).

After the resurrection, Jesus was with the disciples for forty days. He did not tell them how terrible hell was or about the pain and shame He endured on the cross. He had only one subject to talk to them about, the kingdom of God.

> "To whom He also presented Himself alive after His suffering by many infallible proofs, being seen by them during forty days and speaking of the things pertaining to the kingdom of God" (Acts 1:3).

If the kingdom of God is the priority of Jesus, it should be our priority as well.

Jesus Told Us to Pray for the Kingdom to Come

When Jesus taught us to pray, He told us to pray for His kingdom to come and His will to be done on earth as it is in heaven. Why does the kingdom need to come to earth? Because humans cannot survive without a kingdom. He desires to see His kingdom come and His will be done here on earth as it is in heaven.

> "In this manner, therefore, pray: Our Father in heaven, hallowed be Your name. Your kingdom come. Your will be done on earth as *it is* in heaven. Give us this day our daily bread. And forgive us our debts, as we forgive our debtors. And do not lead us into temptation, but deliver us from the evil one. For Yours is the kingdom and the power and the glory forever. Amen" (Matthew 6:9-13).

Jesus Came to Give Us a Kingdom

Many think Jesus came to give us a religion and that Jesus started Christianity, and that it is a better religion than others. He did not come to start a religion, and He never called any of His followers Christians. He came to give us a kingdom.

"Do not fear, little flock, for it is your Father's good pleasure to give you the kingdom" (Luke 12:32).

"And I bestow upon you a kingdom, just as My Father bestowed *one* upon Me" (Luke 22:29).

"He has delivered us from the power of darkness and conveyed *us* into the kingdom of the Son of His love" (Colossians 1:13).

The question is, though Jesus gave us a kingdom, how many of us really know anything about a kingdom or what to do with it?

Jesus Told Us to Preach the Kingdom

When Jesus sent out His disciples He told them specifically what they should preach. They were commanded to preach the kingdom of God.

"And as you go, preach, saying, 'The kingdom of heaven is at hand'" (Matthew 10:7).

No one in the Old Testament could preach what we preach. The kingdom had not arrived then. They were looking forward to the coming of the kingdom, to live in the days that we are living in.

As already stated, Jesus instructed His disciples about the sign of His coming and the end of the age when they asked. Jesus was very specific. He said,

> "And this gospel of the kingdom will be preached in all the world as a witness to all the nations, and then the end will come" (Matthew 24:14).

Jesus Preached the Kingdom of God

Jesus began His earthly ministry by declaring the arrival of the kingdom in Matthew 4:17, and He ended it after His resurrection when He spoke to them about the kingdom of God again in Acts 1:3. He did not preach healing; He preached the kingdom and then healed the sick. He did not preach deliverance; He preached the kingdom and delivered people. He did not preach prosperity; He came with the gospel of the kingdom. There is prosperity in His kingdom.

> "Then Jesus went about all the cities and villages, teaching in their synagogues, preaching the gospel of the kingdom, and healing every sickness and every disease among the people" (Matthew 9:35).

> "But He said to them, 'I must preach the kingdom of God to the other cities also, because for this purpose I have been sent'" (Luke 4:43).

REDISCOVERING THE LOST KINGDOM

There are several schools of thought about the kingdom of God among today's Christians and theologians. Many of them are not biblical. One school of thought says that Jesus preached the kingdom because that is what the Jewish people were waiting for: the liberation of Israel from the rule of Rome, to reestablish them as a kingdom. So to suffice their expectation and to make them happy, Jesus preached the kingdom for three-and-a-half years and no one preached the kingdom after Jesus died. In other words, Jesus was beguiling them by talking about the kingdom, which He was not planning to establish anyway at that time.

The second school of thought says that Jesus came to give the kingdom to Israel but they rejected it, so God postponed it and inserted a parenthetical church age that had not been originally planned. After the church is raptured, the gospel of the kingdom will again be preached (by the Jewish people) during the great tribulation. Both of these are philosophies created academically and are not supported by Scripture.

Jesus came to give them a kingdom, which He stated very plainly in Luke 12:32,

> "Do not fear, little flock, for it is your Father's good pleasure to give you the kingdom."

They did not reject the kingdom; they rejected Jesus. They did not want Him to be their king because He did not fit their idea of how a king would act and live. So Jesus told them He would take the kingdom from them and give it to another nation.

"Jesus said to them, 'Have you never read in the Scriptures: "The stone which the builders rejected has become the chief cornerstone. This was the Lord's doing, and it is marvelous in our eyes"? Therefore I say to you, the kingdom of God will be taken from you and given to a nation bearing the fruits of it'" (Matthew 21:42-44).

The nation to which Jesus refers in this verse is the church. We are called a holy nation in 1 Peter 2:9. The Jewish people were expecting the arrival of their Messiah to restore their kingdom. That part is true. But the type of kingdom God was planning to establish through Jesus at His first coming was not an earthly or physical kingdom, but spiritual. So they rejected Him. The Jewish people did not reject the kingdom. They were waiting and asking for it.

Even after the resurrection the disciples asked Jesus about this.

"Therefore, when they had come together, they asked Him, saying, "Lord, will You at this time restore the kingdom to Israel?" (Acts 1:6).

They were still expecting a natural kingdom. In another place we read:

"Now as they heard these things, He spoke another parable, because He was near Jerusalem and because they thought the kingdom of God would appear immediately" (Luke 19:11).

The parable Jesus shared was about a nobleman going away to a far country to receive for himself a kingdom and then return. He called his servants and gave them his goods to do business until he returned (Luke 19:12-27). That parable is applicable to us today. It is what we are supposed to be doing while we wait for the return of the King.

The kingdom appeared on the day of Pentecost, and it was a spiritual kingdom. When we study the book of Acts, we see that the apostles preached the kingdom of God, especially to the Gentiles. After the arrival of the Holy Spirit, only the disciples understood what kind of kingdom Jesus had been preaching about all those years.

Jesus Preached the Kingdom of God After His Resurrection

"To whom He also presented Himself alive after His suffering by many infallible proofs, being seen by them during forty days and speaking of the things pertaining to the kingdom of God" (Acts 1:3).

Peter Preached the Kingdom of God

What I did not understand for a long time was the message Peter preached on the day of Pentecost. I wondered why he did not mention anything about the kingdom of God in his message. Why was it only about repentance and baptism? I was ignorant and blinded by the religious spirit for a long time and that is why I did not see anything about God's kingdom in his message. To be honest, Peter spoke about repentance and baptism only after people asked him what they should do, after they heard his preaching. The theme of the message he preached prior to that was about David and his throne, and how God raised Jesus to sit on that throne. He preached the kingdom of God from a historical perspective, and showed that Jesus is the fulfillment of the prophecies and promises God gave to David.

Peter preached more about the kingdom of God in that one message than anyone else in the entire book of Acts. He referred to David and his throne several times. What does David have to do with the day of Pentecost? Or the arrival of the Holy Spirit? Or the inauguration of the church? Why would Peter refer to David in the first message ever preached in the Church Age? This gets very interesting. There are ten references to David and nine references to Abraham in the book of Acts.

Remember, Jesus is the Son of David, the legal heir to his throne. God promised David an eternal throne and a kingdom (2 Samuel 7:12-16; Luke 1:31-33).

> "When your days are fulfilled and you rest with your fathers, I will set up your seed after you, who will come from your body, and I will establish his kingdom. He shall build a house for My name, and I will establish the throne of his kingdom forever. I will be his Father, and he shall be My son. If he commits iniquity, I will chasten him with the rod of men and with the blows of the sons of men. But My mercy shall not depart from him, as I took it from Saul, whom I removed from before you. And your house and your kingdom shall be established forever before you. Your throne shall be established forever" (2 Samuel 7:12-16).

Jesus was called the Son of David throughout the gospels. The Holy Spirit gave Peter a revelation about that when

He stood up to preach. It had everything to do with God's eternal kingdom.

When those Jewish people heard that message, they were cut to the heart and ran to him. Jesus said that from the day of John the Baptist, the kingdom of God was being preached and everyone was pressing into it. Three thousand people ran to Peter to get into the kingdom that day.

> "Men *and* brethren, let *me* speak freely to you of the patriarch David, that he is both dead and buried, and his tomb is with us to this day. Therefore, being a prophet, and knowing that God had sworn with an oath to him that of the fruit of his body, according to the flesh, He would raise up the Christ to sit on his throne, he, foreseeing this, spoke concerning the resurrection of the Christ, that His soul was not left in Hades, nor did His flesh see corruption. This Jesus God has raised up, of which we are all witnesses. Therefore being exalted to the right hand of God, and having received from the Father the promise of the Holy Spirit, He poured out this which you now see and hear. For David did not ascend into the heavens, but he says himself:

> 'The Lord said to my Lord,
> "Sit at My right hand,
> Till I make Your enemies Your footstool"'"
> (Acts 2:29-35).

It is interesting to look at how each of the gospels presents the entry of Jesus into Jerusalem. When the people shouted hosanna

in the highest or hosanna to the Son of David, Mark recorded it
with David's kingdom, which we do not see in the other gospels.

"Then those who went before and those who
followed cried out, saying:

'Hosanna!
Blessed *is* He who comes in the name of the Lord!
Blessed *is* the kingdom of our father David that
comes in the name of the Lord!
Hosanna in the highest!'" (Mark 11:9-10).

In His triumphal or royal entry into Jerusalem, He was
fulfilling one of the major prophecies in the Old Testament
because He actually was their King.

"Rejoice greatly, O daughter of Zion! Shout, O
daughter of Jerusalem! Behold, your King is coming
to you; He *is* just and having salvation, Lowly and
riding on a donkey, A colt, the foal of a donkey"
(Zechariah 9:9).

Clearly God did not "insert" the church into His original
plan; the church had been part of His plan all along.

Philip Preached the Kingdom of God to the People of Samaria

"But when they believed Philip as he preached the
things concerning the kingdom of God and the name

of Jesus Christ, both men and women were baptized" (Acts 8:12).

Paul Preached the Kingdom of God and Spoke About Entering It

"Strengthening the souls of the disciples, exhorting *them* to continue in the faith, and *saying,* 'We must through many tribulations enter the kingdom of God'" (Acts 14:22).

"And he went into the synagogue and spoke boldly for three months, reasoning and persuading concerning the things of the kingdom of God" (Acts 19:8).

"And indeed, now I know that you all, among whom I have gone preaching the kingdom of God, will see my face no more" (Acts 20:25).

"So when they had appointed him a day, many came to him at *his* lodging, to whom he explained and solemnly testified of the kingdom of God, persuading them concerning Jesus from both the Law of Moses and the Prophets, from morning till evening" (Acts 28:23).

"Then Paul dwelt two whole years in his own rented house, and received all who came to him, preaching the kingdom of God and teaching the things which concern the Lord Jesus Christ with all confidence, no one forbidding him" (Acts 28:30-31).

When there are that many references to the apostles preaching the kingdom of God, it is difficult to understand why the so-called theologians have a problem approving the message of the kingdom today. It has always been the religious system and the religious spirit that opposes the message of the kingdom of God. When you see someone who does not like the message of the kingdom, it is evidence that a religious spirit is operating in that person. When Jesus was here on earth, the Gentiles and the sinners did not oppose Him or what He preached. It was the religious leaders who opposed Him and did not like what He preached. Some things have not changed.

Our Citizenship

Wherever you were born, you became a citizen of that country by birth. As a citizen, you have certain rights and privileges that a visitor does not have. You can vote, you can buy property, you can work, and you can start businesses. You can be part of the government, and so on.

Why does God want you to be born again? This is a spiritual phenomenon as well as a kingdom phenomenon. The main reason God wants you to be born again is because He wants you to be a citizen of a new country. When you were born again you became a citizen of the kingdom of heaven. That is why Paul says our real citizenship is not on earth, but in heaven (Philippians 3:20). Following are some of the differences between a good Christian and a kingdom citizen, and how they function.

A Good Christian	A Kingdom Citizen
Getting saved and going to heaven are the most important goals in life.	Living as a child of God to make a difference on this earth for Him is the most important goal in life.
Christians live singing that we don't belong here: "When we all get to heaven…"	A Kingdom Citizen lives like their Daddy owns the planet.
A Good Christian pays tithes and gives alms.	Kingdom Citizens create wealth for kingdom purposes.
Christians live to study and find a job to make a living.	Kingdom Citizens discover their purpose and fulfill it.
Christians live to be good and faithful members of a church.	Kingdom Citizens live to execute the will of their heavenly Father.
Christians believe their primary purpose for living is to sing (worship) to God.	A Kingdom Citizen's primary purpose is to see God's will done on earth as it is in heaven
Christians live to see another miracle.	Kingdom Citizens live to study and learn God's ways.
For Christians, Sunday morning is the most spiritual day.	For a Kingdom Citizen, every day is a spiritual day. "This is the day the Lord has made; we will rejoice and be glad in it" (Psalm 118:24).

A Good Christian	A Kingdom Citizen
Christians live to feel the presence of God.	Kingdom Citizens carry and release the presence of God wherever they go.
Christians love their own kind.	Kingdom Citizens love everyone.

Chapter 4: The Most Liberating Message

Chapter 4: The Most Liberating Message

"Your kingdom come. Your will be done on earth
as it is in heaven." Matthew 6:10

Why is the kingdom message the most liberating message in the world?

The kingdom message is God's ultimate solution to every human problem

The kingdom of God has the solution to every problem we will face on earth. The reason you are having challenges in any area of your life is because you are not sure how that part of your life works in His kingdom. It is like a person traveling in a foreign country and not knowing how the system works in that country. For example, in the country that I am from, to use public transportation to go somewhere, you get on a bus and then you buy the ticket to the place you want to go to from the driver. When I went to New York City, I found that the system there worked differently. You need to buy the ticket in advance and then get on the bus. You can get into trouble with the authorities if you do not know how things work. It is the same in the spirit. If you do not know how things work in the kingdom of God, you will have problems. You were born to live in a kingdom.

God saw the earth and how people in it were worried and burdened with the problems of life. He sent His own Son with the solution to all of those problems. The solution is the kingdom of God. The Father told the Son to bring us His kingdom because He saw everyone struggling and dying without it.

It provides man's basic needs. No one needs to live in hunger

There is no need for anyone to live in hunger on this planet. You will read more about this later in this book.

It helps people discover their purpose

You can't discover God's kingdom and not discover your purpose. It is impossible. Your purpose is connected to His kingdom.

It restores human value

Jesus said that if our heavenly Father takes care of and provides for the birds and the lilies of the field, He will surely take care of us because we are more valuable than they. You are valuable to God because you are the King's kid.

It liberates man from poverty

Jesus said He is anointed to preach the gospel to the poor. Why do the poor need the gospel? Because it will bring them back to the kingdom, where they belong. They will discover their purpose and that will be the end of their poverty.

It is the only hope for humanity

The gospel of the kingdom is the only message God gave us to preach. Every other message we preach is a subsidiary of the kingdom, or an aspect of it. He knows the kingdom is the only hope for humanity.

It liberates man from a caste system and racism

As I mentioned, the only message that will unify the people of the world is the message of the kingdom. People are divided based on their country, their race, color, and their language. Although we have been preaching Jesus, even the body of Christ is divided and scattered. Knowing we all belong to the same kingdom (same country) and serve the same King should bring down the walls that divide and separate us.

It allows us to live free from worry

Knowing the kingdom of God is what we need, our Lord Jesus Christ specifically commanded us not to worry. In Matthew 6:25-34, Jesus taught His disciples the secret to worry-free living. They were working men and they had businesses to support their families. When Jesus called them, they left their businesses and followed Him. They did not sell their businesses and collect the savings to support their families for a while. It was a sudden change from having income to support them to having no income the next day. A fishermen's income depended on what they caught each day. If something like that happened in our society, it would be considered shocking. What if the main breadwinner loses his or her job without any warning? Or what if something tragic happens to someone in the family? How does life go on after that?

Of course, life does go on. That is what Jesus was teaching them, how to live without depending on the world system and how to live in His kingdom. His disciples were worried about where the next meal was going to come from and how they were going to support their families. In response to their apprehension, He said,

> "Therefore I say to you, **do not worry** about your life, what you will eat or what you will drink; nor about your body, what you will put on. Is not life more than food and the body more than clothing? Look at the birds of the air, for they neither sow nor reap nor gather into barns; yet your heavenly Father feeds them. Are you not of more value than they? Which of you by worrying can add one cubit to his stature?
>
> "So why do you worry about clothing? Consider the lilies of the field, how they grow: they neither toil nor spin; and yet I say to you that even Solomon in all his glory was not arrayed like one of these. Now if God so clothes the grass of the field, which today is, and tomorrow is thrown into the oven, *will He* not much more *clothe* you, O you of little faith?
>
> "Therefore **do not worry**, saying, 'What shall we eat?' or 'What shall we drink?' or 'What shall we wear?' For after all these things the Gentiles seek. For your heavenly Father knows that you need all these things. But seek first the kingdom of God and His righteousness, and all these things shall be added to you. Therefore **do not worry** about tomorrow, for tomorrow will worry about its own things. Sufficient for the day *is* its own trouble" (Matthew 6:25-34).

Jesus said not to worry three times in that one passage. That means it is very important to Him that we do not worry. When we worry we are not displaying a good witness to the rest of creation that He is a good Father. It leaves a bad impression about His character, and He takes that very personally.

God never intended for you to worry about anything. Worry is a virus from the enemy's kingdom that causes your mind and body to malfunction. Worry-free living is not a mental ascent or euphoric feeling you achieve by repeating some religious mantra. Worry is not part of God's nature or His kingdom. The culture of His kingdom is righteousness, peace, and joy in the Holy Spirit.

It is the knowledge of the *truth about the situation* you are worried about that sets you free from worrying. The Bible says, "My (God's) people are destroyed for lack of knowledge" (Hosea 4:6; Isaiah 5:13).

The lies of the enemy, combined with doubt, bring worry. We tend to worry about things that are out of our control. You are worried about an area of your life because you believe a lie of the enemy and lack the revelation of God over it.

Maybe you heard what God said about worrying, but it has not yet become revelation in your spirit. *Just because you know something does not mean you are benefiting from it.* When the knowledge you have grows into understanding, it becomes revelation. *Revelation is the key to your breakthrough.*

If you worry about money it means you do not know what God says about your finances in His kingdom. To be free from worrying about money, you need an understanding of how God's economic system works. I call it Kingdom Economy.

If you are worried about your health or sick in your body, you are not sure of how the health care system works in His kingdom and most likely, what God says about what you should and should not eat. I call it Kingdom Agriculture.

If you are worried about being able to meet the basic needs of your family, you do not understand the foundational principles of His kingdom and how the King relates to His children.

If you are worried about relationships or family, you are not functioning according to biblical principles for relationship and family. I call it Kingdom Family.

You worry when you are doing something you are not created to do. You worry because of a lack of trust in God. You worry because you want to be in control. When we worry, we question God's faithfulness. *Will He provide? Will He protect? Will He do what He said He would do?* When you are sure of your provision, purpose, and protection, you will stop worrying.

There are three major areas of worry. The majority of people in the world are worried about meeting their basic needs (food, shelter, and clothing). According to UN statistics, at least eighty percent of humanity lives on less than ten dollars a day. Twenty percent live on less than a dollar a day.

The second reason people worry is because they are trying to control a future event that is not here yet. The third reason is regret, wishing they could go back and fix something in the past. Both are impossible. Worry is one of the most futile things you can do; it has no benefit whatsoever, but plenty of side effects. It is also one of the most harmful things you can do to yourself, like smoking or drinking.

Worrying about something won't change anything. To change something, you need to gain new knowledge and take action based on that knowledge. I wish I could regain all the time that I spent worrying in the past. I could have written ten more books! Worrying creates anxiety, which leads to stress—and eventually depression and all sorts of physical problems.

You can be a good Christian and still be broke. You can be a Spirit-filled believer and still not know your purpose. You can be a tongue-talking Jesus follower and be sick in your body. You can be called to ministry and still starve, but when you discover God's kingdom you cannot live broke, sick, hungry, or full of worry anymore. In His kingdom you will find everything you need—healing, provision, peace, purpose, etc.

Jesus used two of His creations to teach us a lesson about worrying. Everything God created reveals an aspect of His glory. He has hidden the laws that govern life and the mysteries of His kingdom in the things He created. That is why when Jesus taught about the mysteries of His kingdom, He used things He created in His parables. In this lesson He used the birds of the air and lilies of the field to teach us the secret behind not worrying.

Jesus' solution for people who were worried about what they were going to eat, drink, and wear was to seek the kingdom of God. That means before we do anything in life, the first thing we need to do is seek His kingdom. He did not say to seek a good church, good education, or a better job. No. He knew that man was worrying about all these things because he'd lost God's kingdom. Those basic necessities are part of His kingdom.

I believe if Jesus were to come today He would preach the same message He preached two thousand years ago. He wouldn't tell you to go to a famous university and get a good education first, so that you will be able to find a good job and make a living. No, He would not.

Is Jesus against getting a good education? He is not. I'm not against it either. What He's saying is that education is not the requirement in His kingdom and that is not how it operates. A person doesn't enter His kingdom based on his or her educational qualifications; His kingdom is made of laws and principles that will work for anyone at any time, in any place. There is definitely a place for education in His kingdom, but that is not the source of our income, provision, value, or significance.

It's possible to be a Christian and not live in the Father's kingdom or know much about it. I was a Christian who lived in lack and scarcity. I went to church three times a week and was forced to fast twice a week. In spite of all that, I didn't know anything about God's kingdom.

Jesus told us to look at the birds of the air. He did not say to look at the birds that are in a zoo or in a cage at a pet store. Why the birds of the air? What does He want us to learn from the birds? Every day they wake up singing. I hear their singing at four o'clock in the morning. Have you ever seen a bird storing up food for the next day? They know tomorrow will take care of itself. Their provision is part of the system God established. If God created something, He knows He is responsible to take care of it.

Birds are created to be in the air. Why is air important to birds? Birds don't "eat" air. Birds need food to eat and air to fly because they are created for it. A bird will never worry about flying. That is their domain. When they are at the place of their *function and purpose,* they are not worried about anything. Everything God created has a place and purpose. Then He said, "Your heavenly Father feeds them. Are you not of more value than they?" (Matthew 6:26).

Can you imagine God feeding the innumerable number of creatures He created—those in the air, in the forest, and in the water—every single day? I have never seen a bird working overtime trying to feed itself and its family. I have been to some of the poorest areas on this earth and still haven't seen a bird hesitant to go home in the evening because it didn't get enough food. But I have seen and read almost daily about thousands of human beings starving and dying of hunger. Statistics say more than twenty thousand people die every day of hunger or hunger-related causes. My question is, "Why?" Doesn't God care about these people more than He cares for the birds?

When the Israelites came out of Egypt, who fed them? The Bible says there were six hundred thousand men and their wives and children! That was probably close to three million people, plus their livestock. God fed them all for *forty years!* He provided manna, meat, and water for them. Imagine how many truckloads of food and water were needed to feed three million people a day! An average family of four needs forty thousand US dollars a year to survive. How much would it cost for six hundred thousand families a year?

The second part of creation Jesus used to teach us not to worry is the lilies of the field. Again, He specified lilies of the *field.* Lilies are created to be in the field. They don't *eat* the field, but it is necessary for their survival. They are not trying to grow and become something. They grow and bring forth their flowers. Have you seen a tree trying to grow, or a lily working hard to produce its flowers? It all happens as part of a natural process.

Why do so many people in this world struggle to meet their basic needs? Many think their number one problem is a lack of food and clothing. They think if they have food and clothing, they have a life. According to Jesus, that is not true. He said, "Is not life more than food and the body more than clothing?" (Matthew 6:25). That means your *life* needs something more important than food and your body is made for something more important than clothing. What could that be? Your life is not meant to be spent working for food or things that perish with use. Jesus said,

> "Do not labor for the food which perishes, but for the food which endures to everlasting life, which the Son of Man will give you, because God the Father has set His seal on Him" (John 6:27).

We have been taught that food and clothing are the number one things we need for survival. But Jesus said He will provide those if we seek something different. People who are alive and have food to eat are not necessarily fulfilling their purpose or living a life of fulfillment. What is the purpose of our body? Our body is made to be the temple of God. This means that our body gives God and our spirit the legal right to operate on the earth. To live and operate on earth requires a physical body. That is why evil spirits look for a body to enter. We have made our body all about eating food and wearing clothing. How sad!

The only creatures that are not happy to be what God created them to be are humans. A bird is happy to be a bird. A tree is happy to be a tree. But if you look at man, he is not happy to be a man. He is trying to be something else. In our society today, there is much confusion about gender. Men are trying to be women and women are trying to be men. Imagine a man confused about which bathroom he should use! Sadly, confusion and chaos have become constants in our society.

Birds are doing what they are born to do. God feeds them, but that does not mean He brings their food to their nests. No, they still have to go and find it. That is their purpose. The lilies are doing what they are created to do. Birds wake up early in the morning, singing about the day, while we are hesitant to wake up at all. Why do many people hate to go to work? Because they know that what they are doing is not what they were born to do.

As I mentioned, everything God created has a place and purpose. Birds need air to fly, fish need water to swim in, and plants need the earth to grow. If you remove a bird from the air, it will not live as God intended. If you remove a fish from the water, it will die. And if you remove a plant from the earth, it too will wither and die.

Is it possible that the reason thousands of humans die every day from hunger and remain hopeless is because they are not in the right place fulfilling their purpose? That is what Jesus said. When He looked at the crowd, He saw that they were all worried about what they were going to eat, drink, and wear. He saw them living like orphans—without a Father or a purpose. You might say that humans are created to live on the earth. Yes, that is true. Then why do these and many more die and remain hopeless? Man needs something more than just earth. If the *air* and *field* is not food for the birds and the lilies, then what is man's "air" and "field"? What I mean is, according to God's perspective, what is required other than food for man to live?

Birds can live in a house or in a cage, but that is not the place of their optimal function and purpose. They are created to be free in the air. Each creation requires an environment for their optimal function. Fish can live in an aquarium, but that is not the place they were created to be. Even different fish require different types, or bodies, of water. Man can live on the earth, but he needs a specific environment for his optimal function and purpose. All plants and creatures do not grow just anywhere; they all require a particular atmosphere.

When God created Adam, he didn't just put him anywhere. The Lord created a very specific environment for him to live and function in. He knew that for this man to function at his full potential, he required something more than just earth. So the Lord planted a garden called Eden. The Bible says God took him and put him in the garden. There is another name for the garden of Eden and that is *the kingdom of God*. He did not take him to the bush or to the jungle, but to a garden. Why?

Every product of value comes with a manual. If you read the manual, the manufacturer clearly mentions the environment that product needs for it to work effectively. It will tell you about the temperature and different conditions that product requires, as well as the environments to stay away from for it to operate as the manufacturer intended. If those conditions are not met the product will malfunction.

Man was created to live in a garden-like environment. When I say garden, I don't necessarily mean a place with flowers and plants. The first thing that comes to my mind when I think of a garden is order and beauty. The Bible says our God is a God of order. He has made everything beautiful. Another thing that comes to my mind is productivity or fruitfulness. The first commandment God gave to man was to be fruitful (Genesis 1:28). If something is not fruitful in a garden, it gets cut down and replaced with something else. A garden needs to be protected, cultivated, and nurtured.

A garden also represents nature. In nature, God hid everything man needed to know concerning Himself and His kingdom. Jesus used things from nature in most of His parables to reveal the mysteries of His kingdom.

> "For since the creation of the world His invisible *attributes* are clearly seen, being understood by the things that are made, *even* His eternal power and Godhead, so that they are without excuse" (Romans 1:20).

> "Then the LORD God took the man and put him in the garden of Eden to tend and keep it. And the LORD God commanded the man, saying, 'Of every tree of the garden you may freely eat'" (Genesis 2:15-16).

"He who did not spare His own Son, but delivered Him up for us all, how shall He not with Him also freely give us all things?" (Romans 8:32).

Though the Bible says that God took Adam to a garden, it means, first of all, that it was a place where the presence or dominion of God was. When Adam lost the garden, he not only lost his food, but most importantly, he lost the presence of God.

Adam's food, shelter, and clothing were already prepared for him. That's the way God's kingdom operates. God will never send you to a place where He hasn't prepared provision for you. He told Elijah to go to Zarephath where He had commanded a widow to provide for him (1 Kings 17:9).

Our God is a King. We are kings with a little "k." Kings require a place of dominion. Every man has the desire to build, cultivate, manage, establish, and rule. If they cannot do those things, they get frustrated. We are designed and created to live in a kingdom. Without a kingdom, man cannot exist- good or evil. Man was created to be a king on the earth and have dominion.

Adam's purpose was to tend and keep the garden. His food and all other needs were included in His purpose—even his wife. God brought her to the garden, the place of his purpose. He didn't have to do a separate "job" to feed himself and his family. Many people are not finding their mate these days because they are not at the place of their purpose.

When Adam disobeyed God, he lost the garden—the environment required for his function and purpose. He began to feel hunger, hopelessness, and worry outside of the garden. As long as Adam was in the garden, he did not lack anything. As long as you are in God's kingdom, you won't lack anything either.

Ever since then, man has been trying to create an environment like the garden with the things of the earth—but it never even comes close. The enemy of man began to offer him luxury, comfort, fun, the pleasures of this world, and all sorts of things to substitute for what he lost. But it never satisfies his soul; instead, it hurts and destroys him in the end.

Adam did not fall from heaven. When he fell he did not lose heaven. He lost a kingdom because his relationship with God was broken. When God decided to save or reconcile man to Himself, He sent His Son with a special gift. He did not come with a bunch of philosophies or theories like other religious leaders. He did not come with a revival message. He brought to man what we lost in the garden. He brought the kingdom of God to us. If God had sent His Son to save fish that were dying without water, He would have sent Him with water. If God were trying to save birds that were dying without air, He would have come with air. He would not come with a philosophy or a religion. That is not what they needed.

Jesus came with one message and He preached it day in and day out. This was the message of the kingdom of God, knowing that it was what people needed the most—people who were full of anxiety over what they were going to eat, drink, and wear. Jesus said, "Seek first the kingdom of God and His righteousness and all these things shall be added to you" (Matthew 6:33; Luke 12:31). Jesus came to give us a kingdom (Luke 12:32; 22:29).

How Does Seeking God's Kingdom Meet Man's Basic Needs?

Instead of taking us all back into a garden, He put His kingdom within us.

> "Now when He was asked by the Pharisees when the kingdom of God would come, He answered them and said, 'The kingdom of God does not come with observation; nor will they say, "See here!" or "See there!" For indeed, the kingdom of God is within you'" (Luke 17:20-21).

God put the garden within us. Now it is up to us to bring His rule and domain wherever we go and through whatever we do. That is the purpose of our existence. We are His garden and He is the Great Gardener. However much of the kingdom of God is inside a person, that much will manifest through the things they do in their life. If the kingdom is not manifesting around you, it's not in you.

People were thinking their main problem was a lack of food, water, and clothing. But in God's sight, that was not their primary problem. Humans were created to live in God's kingdom. Without it they will not survive long, no matter how much money or talent they may have. Just think of some famous and rich people you have heard of who took their own lives or died prematurely.

Every human being on this earth is hungering for one thing: the kingdom of God. But not everyone realizes it because not everyone knows the whole story. Until they discover and find their place in it, they will never be fully satisfied.

In Matthew 6 Jesus said people were hungry, naked, and worried about their life, but not because of a lack of education or employment. They were not in the place God created them to be, so He told them to seek the kingdom of God *first*.

You can be a Christian for many years and still be longing for something. If you are, that means you are not living in God's kingdom yet. Some look for the rapture and many others look for another revival. When you find God's kingdom, you will not long for anything else; you will not long for a revival. Your soul will find its home and you will find rest. That is why Jesus said, "Come to Me, all you who labor and are heavy laden, and I will give you rest" (Matthew 11:28).

Rest does not mean you will not do any more work, but you will be doing a different kind of work, the work your heavenly Father sent you to do. Today, most people don't have any time to do what God created them to do because they are busy trying to provide for themselves.

That is why they hate to go to "work" on Monday morning and can't wait for the next vacation. The majority of the people who are alive on the earth today will live their whole lives and die without ever knowing or fulfilling their purpose. That is why Jesus said to seek His kingdom first, before you do anything with your life.

Why do the poor need to hear the gospel of the kingdom? The poor need food, shelter, and clothing. That is what Jesus said He will provide first when we seek His kingdom.

> "The blind see and the lame walk; the lepers are cleansed and the deaf hear; the dead are raised up

and the poor have the gospel preached to them"
(Matthew 11:5).

Why do the rich need to hear the gospel of the kingdom?
Money won't buy eternal life or an entry into the kingdom of
God. It doesn't matter how much wealth we have; it will not
satisfy us until we discover God's kingdom.

> "And He said to them, 'Take heed and beware
> of covetousness, for one's life does not consist in
> the abundance of the things he possesses'" (Luke 12:15).

We have been preaching the gospel of salvation and people
have been waiting to go to heaven, but they are in debt,
hungry, and broke because they have no revelation of the
kingdom of God. I spent five years in Bible school and did
many other short-term training missions with different
organizations, but I never had a course on the kingdom
of God, the most important message Jesus preached and
commanded us to preach.

God Providing for Our Needs

Why does God want to meet your basic needs? Why is it His
responsibility? When a child is born, it is the responsibility
of the parents to provide for and protect that child. Food,
clothing, shelter, and everything else that child needs will
be provided according to the capacity of the parents. They
provide until that child is grown and mature and able to
support himself. It is the same in God's kingdom.

In His kingdom, He will provide for your basic needs until
you discover your purpose. Then fulfilling your purpose adds

the things you need and want to your life. When you are born again you become a child of God. The first thing you should be seeking after that should be His kingdom, not some religious experience.

He wants to meet our basic needs so we can spend our time doing what He created us to do here. That is why the kingdom message is the most liberating message in this universe. It is not the responsibility of the government of your country to provide for your food. Jesus said our heavenly Father knows that we need all of these things. Our Father knows we need these things, whether we ask for them or not. We don't feed our children because they ask for food. We do it because we know they need it, before they ask.

Most people spend the majority of their time working a "job" to provide for their family. In the kingdom of God, He provides our basic needs so you and I can focus on our purpose. Many people spend excessive hours at their workplace, trying to support their family, just to end up losing their family because they are never home. That is not God's will.

When you are forced to do what you don't like to do, but you have to do it for your survival, it is abuse or slavery. Jesus came to set the captives free. The world's system—or our culture— says money is our biggest problem. To make money, you need to go to school and get an education. Why? When you have an education, you can find a job that helps you make money so you can pay your bills and buy food.

If you ask most people why they work, their reply would be, "to pay bills," or "to buy food," or something similar. Jesus said that if you seek His kingdom first, He will provide your basic needs and help you focus on discovering your purpose.

Once you find your purpose, your provision is included in your purpose. The devil does not want you to know this; neither does he want you to discover your purpose. He wants to keep you religious and busy, looking forward to some spiritual experience that is going to happen some day or in the sweet by-and-by. As long as you are looking forward to experiencing what God has promised in the future, you will never experience it *now*. Faith says, "Now!"

Chapter 5: The Lord's Prayer: Keys to Living In His Kingdom

Chapter 5: The Lord's Prayer: Keys to Living in His Kingdom

"And I will give you the keys of the kingdom
of heaven, and whatever you bind on earth will
be bound in heaven, and whatever you loose on
earth will be loosed in heaven."
Matthew 16:19

Jesus never *taught* His disciples how to heal the sick, how to cast out a demon, or how to prophesy in a classroom setting. Instead, He showed these things in practical lessons. One thing He taught them was how to pray. Most born-again believers do not pray the Lord's Prayer. They think it is a religious prayer. It is not a religious prayer; it is a kingdom prayer. Everything related to our lives is included in the Lord's Prayer. It covers the spiritual, physical, and social aspects of our lives. I did not understand this for a long time. In the following lines I want to explain a little bit about the mysteries hidden in it.

I do not believe we need to pray for His kingdom to come anymore because according to Mark 9:1, the kingdom of God already came with power on the day of Pentecost. Now we need to pray for its manifestation and work to execute the will of God on earth as it is in heaven.

"In this manner, therefore, pray:

Our Father in heaven,
Hallowed be Your name.
Your kingdom come.
Your will be done
On earth as *it is* in heaven.
Give us this day our daily bread.
And forgive us our debts,
As we forgive our debtors.
And do not lead us into temptation,
But deliver us from the evil one.
For Yours is the kingdom and the power and the glory
forever. Amen (Matthew 6:9-13).

Our Father in Heaven

The prayer starts with "our Father in heaven," not "my Father in heaven." It talks about a community or family, telling us that God has more than one child on this planet. The first thing God wants us to know about prayer is that it is a family business, not a religious duty. We need to keep that in our mind as we learn about His kingdom. Sometimes we get so focused on ourselves that we forget that God has other children. He has a big family.

Even though God is a King, we relate to Him as a Father. Why does God want to relate to us as a Father? Some of the major problems in this world today are fatherlessness and father wounds. Many have grown up without a father figure in their lives or with emotional wounds that were inflicted by their fathers or their father figures. Children are supposed to inherit their identity, value, purpose, and destiny from their father.

100

One of the main responsibilities of parenting is to represent and reveal God to our children, and then to guide our children to have a personal relationship with Him. God knew the challenges fathers would face and how the enemy would attack them to confuse children about their identity, value, and purpose. He Himself decided to relate to each human being as their Father.

Once we discover our heavenly Father, we discover our true identity, value, purpose, and destiny. The majority of us did not receive from our fathers what we were supposed to receive. Once you accept God as your heavenly Father, He is the only One who has any right to have any opinion about us, and His is the only opinion we should believe.

Another responsibility of a father is to protect, provide, and teach his children. Children look to their fathers to protect them, provide for them, and teach the lessons of life. Most children feel secure and safe when they are with their father, or when their father is at home. At least, they are supposed to feel that.

The enemy knew that if he could distort the fathers and wound them, then they would not be able to portray God to their children, and the children in turn would never want anything to do with God. It is generally accepted, in both Christian and Therapeutic communities, that most children view God based on the experience they have with their earthly father while growing up.

Hallowed Be Your Name

After we have a revelation of our Father, the second thing He wants us to know about is His name. He wants His name to be made holy on earth and in our lives. What does *holy* mean? The holiness of God is a combination of many of His attributes. Holy means pure. God is pure in all of His dealings with us. It also means without any defilement or blemish. His love, faithfulness, and compassion toward us are pure. He wants His name to be made holy in our lives. He wants us to be pure in all of our dealings because we represent Him on earth. The Bible says that without holiness no man can see God (Hebrews 12:14). Jesus said, "Blessed are the pure in heart, for they shall see God" (Matthew 5:8). Holiness in not an outward expression we obtain by wearing a particular style or color of clothing. Our inner holiness will reflect itself in every aspect of our lives.

What is in His name? Why is God so particular about His name? We know God, and His nature and character, through His names, which are revealed in the Word. Everything He does toward us or for us is a revelation of one of His names. Every miracle in the Bible is a manifestation of one of His names. If He provides for you, that provision is the manifestation of His name, Jehovah Jireh. If He heals you, that is a manifestation of His name Jehovah Rapha. Jesus said in His high priestly prayer in John 17:6a, "I have manifested Your name to the men whom You have given Me out of the world."

Jesus also said that whatever we ask the Father in His name, He will do it for us (John 14:13-14; 15:16; 16:23-24, 26). For every need you have, there is a name of God through which you can access the provision He has in His kingdom.

Your Kingdom Come

It is interesting to note that most Christians are waiting to go to heaven when God's desire and purpose is to bring heaven down to earth, for His kingdom to come on earth. That is His priority. What does it mean to pray for "God's kingdom to come"? What does it look like practically? God never intended for our lives to be any different on earth than in heaven. He wants us to have the same quality of life right now. Does everyone experience that? No.

God created man to live in His kingdom. He knows that man cannot survive without it, and He wants to give it to His children. He also wants us to live on earth depending on His kingdom, not on this world. He wants us to influence earth with heaven. The earth is limited, and His kingdom is unlimited. Earth is natural, and His kingdom is spiritual. We are natural and spiritual at the same time. We are a spirit living in a body.

God is the Creator and the original Owner of this planet. He created it to extend His kingdom, but it was overtaken by the enemy and He has been in the process of reclaiming it. That is why He told us to pray for His kingdom to come here once again. We are the only agents through which that vision can materialize. Jesus came and taught us the principles and mysteries of His kingdom and about how to administer and operate it.

We have not fully gotten hold of God's vision yet. Most of us don't even pray the prayer He taught us to pray. This prayer must be prayed by all of God's children worldwide. Imagine more than a billion saints across the world praying that prayer. Do you know why the Roman Catholic Church has the influence they have? They don't speak (at least most) in tongues and roll on the floor, but they pray that prayer almost every time they meet.

When we pray for His kingdom to come we are praying for His rule, His system of operation, His dominion to come to earth and to every area of our lives; for His kingdom to come in our personal lives, family, finances, etc.; for kingdom economy to come to our finances; for kingdom family to come to our marriages; for kingdom agriculture to come to our eating habits; and for kingdom culture to come to our way of doing things. Each area of our life needs to come under the influence of His kingdom.

Your Will Be Done on Earth as It Is in Heaven

Every king has a will and a plan and wants to see it accomplished in his kingdom. God is a King and His will is accomplished in heaven, as He wants it to be. But on earth, there has been opposition, and someone else's will is being accomplished instead. Right now, in most parts of the earth, Satan's will is accomplished instead of God's. Some people say that God's sovereignty rules everywhere. That is partially true. He has the final say on everything, but if that were entirely true then He would not have told us to pray for His will to be done here as it is in heaven because it would already have been made manifest.

You and I are part of that team to see God's will accomplished on earth as it is in heaven. The church is supposed to be teaching and training people in how to do that, instead of teaching them to sing. We need to learn what God's will is and how He does it in heaven, and copy that on earth. God has a will and plan for every area of our lives. When we deviate from that, we will encounter enormous problems.

There is no poverty, lack, or sickness in heaven because it is not the King's will to have them in heaven. They did not originate in heaven. They are the works of the devil. That is why the Bible says the Son of God was manifested to destroy the works of the devil (1 John 3:8).

As I mentioned earlier, God put man in Eden originally where His will was done as it was in heaven. Then it was man's task to duplicate, expand, and make the entire earth like Eden: to cause the entire earth to be filled with God's kingdom and glory. We failed in that task, and through Jesus He restored that kingdom back to us. Then He gave that assignment to the church: to go and preach the gospel of the kingdom, and to fill the earth with the knowledge of His glory.

The Word of God is the revealed will of God. Whatever the Word says we are, that is what we are, and whatever the Word says we should have, that is what we should have. Whatever the Word says we should do, that is what we should be doing.

Give Us This Day Our Daily Bread

In a kingdom, it is the king's responsibility to take care of the citizens, to make sure everyone has enough to eat and that they are protected. If a citizen of a kingdom is poor, that affects the reputation of the king. God our King guarantees our daily provision, so we should not be worrying about it. The only thing you and I need to make sure of is that we are citizens of His kingdom. You could be a member of a church and not be a citizen of His kingdom. That is a sad dilemma because most people think that because they go to church on Sunday morning they are automatically citizens of God's kingdom. The first requirement for becoming a citizen of God's kingdom is to become a child of the King. Whatever we need for our daily life is called "bread" in the Bible. There are different kinds of bread. I will mention a few of them here:

Natural Food

First, we all need physical bread, or food, every day. God is faithful and is committed to providing that for us. He feeds the birds and animals in the forest, so how much more will He take care of His own children?

"He causes the grass to grow for the cattle, and vegetation for the service of man, that he may bring forth food from the earth, and wine *that* makes glad the heart of man, oil to make *his* face shine, and bread *which* strengthens man's heart" (Psalm 104:14-15).

Jesus promised to provide everything we need if we seek His kingdom first. He promised to provide food and all the other basic provisions we need in our lives. If anyone out there is lacking the basics for their lives, that means they are not seeking His kingdom first.

Healing

Healing is called "bread" in the Bible. There are many viruses and sicknesses our body fights each day, keeping us safe from them. If it were not for our immune system, which is God's healing system in our body, we all would have died. We need healing every day of our lives.

Jesus called healing "the children's bread":

"And behold, a woman of Canaan came from that region and cried out to Him, saying, 'Have mercy on me, O Lord, Son of David! My daughter is severely demon-possessed.' But He answered her not a word. And His disciples came and urged Him, saying, 'Send her away, for she cries out after us.' But He answered and said, 'I was not sent except to the lost sheep of the house of Israel.' Then she came and worshiped Him, saying, 'Lord, help me!' But He answered and said, 'It is not good to take the children's bread and throw *it* to the little dogs.' And she said, 'Yes, Lord, yet even the little dogs eat the crumbs which fall from their masters' table.' Then Jesus answered and said to her, 'O woman, great *is* your faith! Let it be to you as you desire.' And her daughter was healed from that very hour" (Matthew 15:22-28).

Financial Bread

We need money as long as we live on this earth. Money is also called "bread" in the Bible.

"Cast your bread upon the waters, for you will find it after many days" (Ecclesiastes 11:1).

The word "bread" here refers to financial investments.

God is faithful to provide us with the money we need to live. One of the best examples is when Peter wanted to pay the tax. Jesus told him to go and cast the hook, and in the mouth of the first fish would be a piece of money to cover the tax (Mathew 17:27; 2 Corinthians 9:10).

Spiritual Bread

Just like our body needs food to survive, our spirit needs spiritual food for its nourishment and growth. Jesus is called the Bread of Life (John 6:48). In the same way we eat natural food every day, we need to eat the Word every day.

Emotional Bread

We all have emotional needs too. Our heavenly Father is faithful to meet our emotional needs. His love, acceptance, and comfort keep our souls emotionally healthy. God is a Shepherd, meeting our physical, emotional, and spiritual needs (Psalm 23; Psalm 51:12).

We need favor, ideas, wisdom, solutions, and guidance. Every day we need to thank God for providing us with our *daily bread* in all the previously mentioned areas of our lives.

And Forgive Us Our Debts As We Forgive Our Debtors

Everything in God's kingdom flows through relationship. Walking in love and forgiveness is imperative for living in God's kingdom. We are commanded to forgive others as He forgives us. If we do not forgive others God will not forgive us our sins; it is that important. God forgiving our sins is conditional on us forgiving others. That sounds a little scary to me. Jesus taught on forgiveness more than once. Some examples are Matthew 18:21-35 and Mark 11:25-26. There will be some people in your life who are hard to forgive. Whenever you pray this prayer, mention their names and release forgiveness from your heart.

And Do Not Lead Us into Temptation

Every sin originates with a temptation. The enemy is lurking to tempt us every chance he gets. Our great-grandparents, Adam and Eve, were tempted and fell into transgression and sin entered the world. Jesus was tempted by the enemy, but He overcame it. We are supposed to follow the footsteps of our Lord and overcome temptations. We are prone to be tempted and we need the grace of God each day to walk in victory.

The evil one will set snares on our way to trap us in his net. We read in Psalm 91:3a:

> "Surely He shall deliver you from the snare of the fowler."

It is a promise from our heavenly Father to deliver us from those snares.

But Deliver Us From the Evil One

The Bible says the enemy is walking around like a roaring lion to find whom he may devour (1 Peter 5:8). We need to ask God daily to deliver us from the evil one, who is Satan and his works. What are his works? Poverty, debt, curses, sicknesses and diseases, strife, offenses, delays, stealing, fear, deception, lies are some of his works. If any of the abovementioned works are operating in your life, ask the Lord to remove and deliver you from the works of the evil one. He will do it if you ask Him. For the Son of God was manifested to destroy the works of the evil one (1 John 3:8). I have paraphrased the Lord's Prayer and mentioned it below, so that you can pray it every day before you start your day. If you do you will notice the difference.

For Yours Is the Kingdom and the Power and the Glory Forever!

The kingdoms of this world, with their power and glory, belong to our God. The enemy stole that from Him through man; and when Jesus was tempted, the devil offered Him the world, its kingdoms, and its glory (Luke 4:5-7). Since the enemy took it from us, God wants to restore it through us. That is why Jesus died for our sins. We have been taught that Jesus died to recruit and take a bunch of people to heaven. As the Bible says, sin came through man, and salvation from sin also came through a Man, Jesus Christ (Romans 5:12-17).

If there is any area of your life that is not in alignment with the kingdom of God, you have the right and opportunity now to bring it back into alignment, whether it is your finances, health, family life, children, your community and nation, or anything else. As a kingdom ambassador, this is your responsibility. There has been reconciliation between heaven and earth, things in heaven and things on earth, through the blood of Jesus (Ephesians 1:7-10; Colossians 1:19-22). Whenever you see something that is not in alignment with God's will, you need to release kingdom authority by commanding (decreeing and declaring) it back into alignment.

I would encourage you to pray the Lord's Prayer whenever you can. If you are part of an *Ekklesia*, when you come together, pray this prayer as a group. I have paraphrased the prayer for you below. You are free to personalize it as the Holy Spirit leads you:

Our Father in heaven, hallowed be Your name.

Let Your name be made holy in our nation, in my family, and in the whole earth. Thank You for giving us Your kingdom. Help us to administer it effectively on earth. Teach us how to tap into your kingdom resources to solve problems on this earth.

Let Your kingdom rule and dominion come into my life, family, and nation.

Let Your kingdom economy, culture, education, and health come to this earth, in my life, nation, and family.
Your will be done on earth as it is in heaven.
Give us this day our daily, physical, financial, spiritual, and emotional bread.
And forgive us our debts,
As we forgive our debtors.

(If there is anyone you need to forgive, say their name and release forgiveness from your heart.)
And do not lead us into temptation,
But deliver us from the evil one.

Thank You for protecting us from evil, curses, offenses, jealousy, strife, sickness, ignorance, lack, and poverty.
For Yours is the kingdom and the power and the glory forever. Amen.

Chapter 6: Life in the Kingdom

Chapter 6: Life in the Kingdom

"For the kingdom of God is not eating and
drinking, but righteousness and peace and joy in
the Holy Spirit." Romans 14:17

How much time did Jesus or the disciples spend doing
something to provide for themselves? To my knowledge,
none. Jesus was busy doing what His Father sent Him to do
and the provision was included with His work. How did
Moses support himself and his family when he was sent to
Egypt to deliver the Israelites?

Jesus was training the disciples how to live in His kingdom.
After the training He sent them out to preach. He gave them
"gifts": the power and authority to heal sicknesses, cast out
demons, cleanse the lepers, and raise the dead. When He sent
them out, He specifically told them not to take any money
or any other provision with them. Why? Because He wanted
them to trust Him, and for His kingdom to provide for them.

Remember, your provision is in your purpose. That is the way
the work of the kingdom must be done. This revelation will
revolutionize how we do ministry and mission work today.
Each minister/missionary should receive this revelation before
they go out to preach the gospel. It is a truth that needs to
be taught.

> "Provide neither gold nor silver nor copper in your money belts, nor bag for *your* journey, nor two tunics, nor sandals, nor staffs; for a worker is worthy of his food" (Matthew 10:9-10).

When they came back from the trip, Jesus asked them if they lacked anything. They said they did not.

> "And He said to them, 'When I sent you without money bag, knapsack, and sandals, did you lack anything?' So they said, 'Nothing'" (Luke 22:35).

I heard someone say this would only work in the Jewish culture. That is not true. This will work anywhere in the world. Kingdom principles and culture are universal.

Then, I noticed something very interesting. After Jesus asked them if they lacked anything when He sent them out, and their reply was "nothing," He told them,

> "But now, he who has a money bag, let him take *it,* and likewise a knapsack; and he who has no sword, let him sell his garment and buy one. For I say to you that this which is written must still be accomplished in Me: 'And He was numbered with the transgressors.' For the things concerning Me have an end" (Luke 22:36-37).

Why would Jesus say something like that? It seems as if He is contradicting Himself. They were still in the Jewish culture. What He was saying was that as long as He was with them the kingdom was also with them, and their needs would be provided for by the kingdom. He was going to be taken from them for a few days and they would not enjoy kingdom living for that time period. The kingdom would arrive universally only after His resurrection and ascension—once the Holy Spirit came. Until then, they would need to support themselves. That's why He told them to take money and other material things. That's also the reason Peter went back to fishing—he had no other means of supporting himself. That's why Jesus did not rebuke Peter for what He did. When the Holy Spirit came and the kingdom of God began to operate on the earth, they never returned to do anything to support themselves, even in the midst of severe persecution or famine. They were in the kingdom of God, and the kingdom of God was within them.

When we are born into His kingdom, every one of His children receives one or more gifts (spiritual and natural). When they develop and use them for His kingdom purpose, they will prosper. Usually your natural gift will pave or open the way to your place of your purpose.

God will never ask you to do something for Him without ordaining the provision. That is not the kind of God we serve. People all over the world are crying and saying, "God told me to do this, but I don't have the money to do it." That is not the way His kingdom operates. When the king in a kingdom assigns you to do something for him, he will always make sure the provision is made available to you to fulfill that assignment.

How Do We Seek God's Kingdom?

How do we seek His kingdom? If Jesus had said, "I want you all to seek first the United Kingdom," it would have been easy for us. We would book our ticket and fly to the UK. The kingdom of God is an invisible kingdom. It does not come with observation. We seek God's kingdom mainly in prayer. How each person discovers the kingdom varies from person to person. This is an individual thing, just like salvation. Just because I discovered God's kingdom doesn't mean my children will enter it.

When I was growing up, I was taught that seeking the kingdom meant preaching the gospel or getting baptized. Many people that I know entered into ministry without being called to do it. They misinterpreted "seeking His kingdom" as "being in ministry." That was far from the truth. As a result, I have seen hundreds of believers and pastors living in hunger and lack. I wondered if our God is really a good God. When He opened my eyes to see what He really meant by seeking His kingdom, everything changed in my life.

Some others think seeking God's kingdom means to get closer to God. How do we get closer to a person who is already living in us? If you are born again, Christ lives in you and you are a temple of God. Many others misinterpret it as going to heaven when they die. We will not be seeking anything after we die.

There is no secret formula that can be applied for everyone. It is individual. When you seek his kingdom with all your heart you will find it. The message of the kingdom frees your life from everything the enemy has imposed on you.

When you seek God's kingdom, the primary thing that will happen to you is that you will discover your purpose. Why do the majority of people on earth not know why they exist? It is because they are outside God's kingdom. When you discover your purpose, you will find out that your provision is included in your purpose. That is why Jesus said in Matthew 7:21,

> "Not everyone who says to Me, 'Lord, Lord,' shall enter the kingdom of heaven, but he who does the will of My Father in heaven."

There are so many religious people on earth today who call Jesus their Lord, but their basic needs are not met. Some of them identify themselves as Christians, Pentecostals, or by the name of other various religious denominations.

When you pray and seek His kingdom, God will put a vision in your heart—we call it a dream,, the will of God, passion, or some other title. The Bible says God's people perish only for two reasons: lack of knowledge and lack of vision (Hosea 4:6; Proverbs 29:18 KJV). A vision is a picture of your future that has not materialized yet. Once you receive a vision from God for your purpose, then over the next five years you need to focus your entire life in learning everything about it and its related subjects. That is the way you prepare.

Some visions or dreams may require you to go to a college or university to earn a degree in that subject. If you want to become a medical doctor, lawyer, politician, or work in any other profession, it is imperative that you go to school. No one will become a medical doctor just by revelation alone. If you do, either no one will come to you for treatment, or you will end up in prison! In the kingdom your vision is very important. If you don't have a vision, you are not in the kingdom—you won't go anywhere with your life and God cannot provide for you.

Your vision, dream is God's way—or system—of providing for you in His kingdom. If you seek God's kingdom I can guarantee that you will find it. Once you discover God's kingdom you will find your purpose. That is what God intends for every human being. The reason the majority of the people on this earth do not know their purpose is because they are not in God's kingdom. They are not taught to seek it. I also want to warn you not to make the mistake of trying to *make* it all happen on your own. If you try to make your life happen, you will surely fail. You need to be led by God.

When you discover exactly who you are, whose you are, and exactly what you are supposed to be doing—and constantly live in that awareness—then you won't be worrying. Jesus' solution for worry is not more fun, watch some movies, and eat some ice cream, but to discover His kingdom and your purpose in it.

There are millions of people who are slaves to a system in which they are not happy or satisfied, and there are millions of people who go hungry every day. The preaching of the kingdom is the solution to both these problems. That is why Jesus told us to go and preach the gospel of the kingdom. The gospel is not just for taking people to heaven. The word *gospel* means "good news." Good news to a person who is hungry is food. Good news to a poor person is freedom from poverty. Good news to a person who is naked is clothing. Good news to a person who is bound is deliverance. This gospel of the kingdom needs to be applied to every aspect of our life and society. It is the solution for every human problem.

The Kingdom of God Versus Other Governments

No matter what nation they are in, people are not happy with their government. Failed governments are a universal problem. As Christians, we cannot function without a government either. Jesus came with a government, which is His kingdom. Men have established different forms of government on earth, but they all failed. When Isaiah prophesied about Jesus, the first thing he prophesied about was a government.

> "For unto us a Child is born, unto us a Son is given; and the government will be upon His shoulder. And His name will be called Wonderful, Counselor, Mighty God, Everlasting Father, Prince of Peace. Of the increase of *His* government and peace *there will be* no end, upon the throne of David and over His kingdom, to order it and establish it with judgment and justice from that time forward, even forever. The zeal of the LORD of hosts will perform this" (Isaiah 9:6-7).

God wants His government (kingdom) to come to this earth and to our lives. In His kingdom there is no poverty, sickness, curse, unemployment, hunger, no evil thing. Every form of government on this earth promises good things to the people at first, but in the end it oppresses and kills them. That is the goal of every government initiated by the kingdom of darkness.

Earthly governments don't work. It doesn't matter what type they are. People everywhere are blaming their government for all the turmoil and confusion in their countries, whether it is communist China; India, the largest democracy; or the capitalistic society in the United States—all forms of worldly government are failing men. They were never intended to satisfy mankind. People in every nation are looking for a better government. The only type of government that will satisfy humans is the kingdom of God. When we discover God's kingdom and learn to live in it, we will stop blaming our earthly government.

Jesus came and put the kingdom of God within us (Luke 17:20-21). Wherever we go we carry the most powerful government in the universe inside of us: the kingdom of God, the government of heaven. Jesus said,

"The kingdom of God is within you" (Luke 17:21).

Most people do not know what to do with it or how to exercise its influence to bring any change to their situations.

Ever since man lost the kingdom of God, the devil began to introduce different forms of government and kingdoms on this earth. The first one was the kingdom of Nimrod in Genesis 10:8-10. He was the first superhero on the earth. His intention was to satisfy the longing of men's hearts. There have been many kingdoms and different forms of government, but none of them solved human problems. The reason for all the corruption and abuse in this world is that man is not sure how to provide for his basic needs, so people lie, cheat, and steal to accumulate wealth. There is only one solution to all of the corruption—the kingdom of God. When people discover the kingdom, everything they need will be added to them so they do not need to lie, cheat, and steal from others.

That is why Jesus taught about the kingdom more than anything else. It was the most important thing He needed to communicate. Another thing I've noticed is that humans need to be taught everything. Though we are the most intelligent creatures God created, we still need to be taught. When a baby is born, they need to be taught what to eat or not eat, how to walk, how to speak, and basic hygiene. Then around five or six years of age, they go to school and spend the next twelve or more years learning about the world system. What if we spent two years of our life seeking God's kingdom? What would happen to us if we did?

How Did I Discover the Kingdom of God?

I grew up in a middle-class family in India. My father worked for the government and my mother stayed home and took care of us. The salary my father received was not enough to cover all the needs at home. Every month when he received his salary and paid the bills, within three days there was no money left. I remember my mother sending me to my neighbor's houses to borrow rice, sugar, and sometimes money. I would tell them we would pay it back when my father got paid the next month. I slept on the concrete floor for eighteen years on a single mat without a mattress. We were three brothers and we longed to have a bicycle. When we were teenagers, our father bought a bicycle that we had to share between the three of us.

It was a requirement in our home to fast twice a week. On Friday and Sunday mornings there was no breakfast. My mother became sick and passed away when she was fifty-one years old. I began to wonder what was wrong with our spirituality. If we served the Almighty God, why could He not even meet our basic needs?

I grew up in a very religious church. Everything I did was performance based: to please God or buy His acceptance through what I did (without knowing that He already accepted me and was pleased with me because of what Jesus did). I used to clap my hands so hard that it broke the skin and bled, trying to make God happy, not knowing that He was already happy.

Though we had hundreds of churches of all denominations in my small town, not even that town was fully reached with the gospel. The churches were competing against each other, instead of working together to reach the people. The gospel originally reached India through the apostle Thomas, but the nation of India was not impacted by the gospel, even after almost two thousand years.

Most Christians and ministers that I knew were broke and sick, but they all sang and preached about Jesus coming back soon to take us all "home" so "get ready." It was a "pie in the sky" or "sweet bye-and-bye" gospel they preached. They had nothing to offer for the very real problems the people or nation were facing. I felt there was something wrong with the message we were preaching because it was not working. Jesus did not preach a "pie in the sky" or "who wants to go to heaven?" gospel.

In almost every meeting, they were waiting or hoping for God to show up and fix everything in their lives as well as the problems in the world. They also did not realize that Jesus had already come to fix things for us. At the second coming, He is not coming to fix things, but to reign. Jesus Christ coming in the flesh and walking among men was the greatest manifestation of God on this earth. He came to fix everything that was wrong with humanity. He came to fix the sin problem, which is the root of all the other problems we have. He came to fix the sickness, poverty, and relationship problems. They interpreted it as Him coming to take us all to heaven when we die.

The gospel seemed powerless to change anything in the culture or in people's lives. Everybody was hiding behind a religious mask. They claimed they were saved and holy, but they lacked the understanding of what they were saved from. They had no evidence to show of their salvation. Then, by the grace of God, I entered into ministry, and pretty soon I was frustrated about that too because there were no resources available to do anything God called me to do. The land, and the resources God put in it, are used mostly by the devil and his children.

I was taught that they were not meant for me to use now. I was told that I was created to live in heaven singing for thousands of years. I was not good at singing, so I could not imagine what God would think of my singing to Him for thousands of years. I was really disappointed that He did not give me a good singing voice, in fact. Maybe He did not love me enough! This is what I thought, and it created even more insecurity in me.

Then I came to the West and saw all its glitter and glamour. Everything is about being successful and having fun. I found the resources I was lacking, available in plenty, but behind that fun and success I saw broken lives and families and I realized the fun and success are really a cover-up, a distraction from what is real. People do not know their purpose. They are not fulfilled though they have material abundance. They are raised to believe the sole purpose of life is to get an education and find a nice job, to make some money and have some fun. All the people who had fun by fulfilling the lust of their flesh feel broken and depressed in the latter part of their life.

Almost all of their houses and possessions are owned by banks, so they are enjoying the temporary falsehood of having things without really owning anything. They live and work most of their lives to pay for some pieces of wood and metal. I said to myself: *There is something wrong with this system. There should be something more worth living and dying for.*

The only one good thing about me was that I was honest enough in my younger years to admit that what I believed and did was not working for me or for the people I was trying to help. Most people are not honest with themselves because of pride or ignorance. For some, their religious beliefs bind them, so they live a lie, deceiving themselves and wasting a precious lifetime.

That's when I heard the message of the gospel of the kingdom. It hit me like a bullet, and I knew something had happened in my spirit. There was a shift in my being. But it was a seed that had been planted in me. That seed began to germinate and grow day by day and year by year. Just like Jesus said, the kingdom of heaven is like a mustard seed; though it is one of the smallest of all seeds, when it grows it becomes a very large tree where birds of the sky and animals of the field come to rest (Matthew 13:31-32). I felt like the man who found the pearl of great price, or the man who found the greatest treasure in a field. I did not know everything about it but there was an inner satisfaction. I felt like I was home and belonged for the first time, and that I had a purpose to fulfill.

For a long time, I was afraid to present what I knew because of the fear of people and because of the religious spirit, so I hid the message of the kingdom for almost fifteen years! I wasn't sure if it was the right message. I also needed to mature in it and know what I was preaching. It had to work for me first before I offered it to others. The Lord brought my attention back to His kingdom a couple of years ago. I discovered that the kingdom of God message was the only message Jesus and the apostles preached, and it is the only message that works to solve the problems this world is facing.

How It All Unfolded

When I was sixteen, God put a desire in my heart along with my brother and two other friends of ours to meet and pray. We met once a week at our church building to pray. We prayed from 8:30 in the evening until 4:30 in the morning. We continued that week after week. We were not praying for our personal needs. Our prayers were focused on world evangelism. We prayed for every nation and we dreamed of God using us in mighty and powerful ways. Something began to happen in our spirits—God began to put desires in our hearts that weren't there before. Though we couldn't afford

127

to rent a bicycle for an hour for one penny, He began to put desires that had no possibility of happening in the natural.

When God gave us those desires, we wrote them down on paper and prayed over them. We commanded them to manifest in the natural. Sometimes we drew pictures of the things He was showing us. We got so excited that we would run, jump, and shout for joy because of what God showed us in our spirit. Nothing changed in the natural for a long time. We didn't know we were seeking the kingdom of God. I never heard a message on God's kingdom in our church. God was supernaturally causing us to seek His kingdom. He caused me to discover His kingdom at a very young age. The prayers we prayed then are now being fulfilled in our lives.

Through those prayer meetings God released His kingdom in my heart. It came in the form of a vision, dream, desire, or passion to do something. God was revealing my purpose to me. When you seek His kingdom, your purpose will be birthed in your heart/spirit by the Holy Spirit as a picture or desire. You need to follow that blue print He is showing you. Do not look to the left or right. Everything in the natural will look opposite and impossible to what He has shown you. You need to learn to walk by faith and not by sight.

I began to live not based on my natural circumstances or resources that were available. I started to learn how to tap into the supernatural or unlimited resources of heaven to meet my needs and how to fulfill the vision He put in my heart. The vision God gave you and your ability to articulate it in faith, is the channel by which you connect to the supernatural (kingdom) resources.

If you remove man from the place and purpose God created him, he will get sick and die. A man called me after listening to my teaching about the kingdom on our radio program and said, "Brother Abraham, how can this kingdom teaching help a homeless man living under a bridge in downtown Denver? Don't you think he needs a sandwich first before he hears the teaching on the kingdom?" I replied, "The teaching of the kingdom is exactly what he needs. If our heavenly Father feeds millions of creatures every day, imagine the size of His feeding program. So, why do men and women who are created in His image go hungry and die of starvation?"

Jesus did not tell hungry people to seek first a sandwich and then His kingdom. No, He said to first seek His kingdom and then a sandwich will be added as a bonus. The religious spirit has messed us up so much through wrong teaching that we don't even know how to think right. I told this brother the first thing Jesus promised if we seek His kingdom is a *sandwich* (food and clothing), not heaven.

The real problem is not the hunger problem, nor the homeless problem. *The real problem is the fatherless problem.* Those homeless people do not know that they have a heavenly Father who loves them and wants to take care of them. Many of us are like the Prodigal Son who left his father's house and stayed in a pigpen like a slave, not even having enough to eat. Whose problem was it really? Was it because there was no food in his father's house that he was starving? If he had stayed long enough with the pigs he would have died. Whose problem was it, his or his father's? It was definitely his. We could not blame the father for his death or his starvation. He was experiencing the consequences of his own choice. He was always welcome to go back to his father's house. We need to find what prompts people to choose to leave their Father's house, and what hinders them from returning to their Father's house.

Thank God that he came to himself and had a revelation. He asked himself how many of his father's hired servants had plenty of food to eat and some left over. And here he was: even though he was a son, he was starving for food. Many people today are like that son. Though God feeds millions of creatures every day, many of His own children live in hunger. That is not His will. Whether a person lives under a bridge or in a palace, the first thing they need to do is seek God's kingdom.

The older brother of the Prodigal Son wasn't any better than a servant either. Though he was a son and heir of everything his father owned, he never enjoyed or benefited from his father's wealth. Though many are God's children, not very many are benefiting from what their Father owns.

Galatians 4:1 says,

> "Now I say *that* the heir, as long as he is a child, does not differ at all from a slave, though he is master of all."

That is the problem with most of the children of God. We have immense resources that have been made available to us because our Father owns it all, but many of us are struggling to meet our basic needs. That's not right—and it's not the way we should be living. The reason is because we do not understand our purpose.

Chapter 7: Entering the Kingdom of God

Chapter 7: Entering the Kingdom of God

"Therefore, brethren, be even more diligent to
make your call and election sure, for if you do
these things you will never stumble; for so an
entrance will be supplied to you abundantly into
the everlasting kingdom of our Lord and Savior
Jesus Christ." 2 Peter 1:10-11

When you are born again, you will only *see* the kingdom;
the next step is to *enter* it, as it says in (John 3:3-5).
The first thing we should teach others after they are born again
is about the kingdom and how it operates. Now, you may
ask in your heart how someone can discover the kingdom
or why the majority of Christians missed the message of the
kingdom for so long. Let me be honest with you; the devil
hates the message of the kingdom. As long as the church
keeps preaching about revival, the end times (which we have
been doing for so long), faith, and the rapture, the devil will
not bother much, nor he will not lose much. The moment
you talk about the kingdom of God, you will get his reaction.
He doesn't want to see it manifest on the earth or lose an inch
of this planet to another kingdom.

Satan has different spirits; some are more powerful than
others. He has his levels of authority in his kingdom, as we
read in Ephesians 6:12. Two of those powerful spirits are the

religious spirit and the spirit of this world (1 Corinthians 2:12). When people are deceived by either of these spirits, they will never discover the kingdom of God. These spirits are the antithesis to the Holy Spirit.

When the religious spirit is operating in a person, it makes them feel as though they are so spiritual doing all the Christian duties, keeping the law, and speaking *Christianese*. They will look pious on the outside, but inside it's like a whitewashed tomb. Their religiosity will not benefit them or others. Remember the story of Nicodemus, the religious leader and teacher of Israel, how he did not know anything about the kingdom though he was a ruler? (John 3:1-10). If you would like to know more about the religious spirit and its symptoms, and how to be free from it, please read *Kingdom Secrets to Restoring Nations Back to God*.

The spirit of this world works opposite to the religious spirit. This spirit will offer you all the fun and entertainment you want. Its mission is to keep you busy and distracted. The moment you are done with one event or form of entertainment, it will offer you the next. Something new will always arrive on the market, or the new season of something you enjoy will come. When one distraction is over there will be another. It will keep you blinded and busy, enjoying this world and its glitter so that you will never understand the kingdom of God. It will make you feel you are in the kingdom of God because of all the fun you are having and you are going to church every Sunday.

The third reason people do not discover the kingdom of God is because of pride and self-reliance. Do you remember the first line of the Beatitudes? "Blessed are the poor in spirit, for theirs is the kingdom of heaven" (Matthew 5:3). Here the word "poor" doesn't mean someone without any money. It means someone who is humble, needy, and hungry for God. That is the first condition necessary to receive the kingdom; admitting that you need help. To be honest with you, that is the most difficult thing for some people to admit because they are full of themselves and full of pride. They will not enter the kingdom of God.

That is why Jesus said, "And again I say to you, it is easier for a camel to go through the eye of a needle than for a rich man to enter the kingdom of God" (Matthew 19:24).

Why did Jesus say it is difficult for rich people, or those who think they are rich, to enter the kingdom of God? It is very difficult for them to admit the need for a savior or that they need help from someone else. Their motto is self-reliance, and they would rather do everything by themselves or not do it at all. You need to experience deliverance from the abovementioned spirits before you can enter and experience the kingdom of God.

There are seven principles mentioned in the New Testament about entering the kingdom:

1) Matthew 5:20

> "For I say to you, that unless your righteousness exceeds the righteousness of the scribes and Pharisees, you will by no means enter the kingdom of heaven."

Jesus said, "But seek first the kingdom of God and His righteousness, and all these things shall be added to you." The above Scripture says that unless our righteousness exceeds the righteousness of the Pharisees we shall not enter the kingdom. The Pharisees were one of the most religious Jewish sects in

Jesus' time. They would swallow an elephant in an attempt to filter a mosquito. That means they followed the letter of the Law to its fullest extent and lost the whole purpose behind it, which was to show grace and mercy to the people.

They believed in their own righteousness based on works, and how they looked and what they said. They gave tithes to the temple on everything they possessed. They would not walk by a leper fearing they would become unclean. The lived and died the Old Testament Law like no one else could. Now, Jesus says, our righteousness has to exceed theirs to enter into His kingdom. What does that mean? Do we have to do more righteous works? Do we have to follow the Law more strictly than they did? Do we have to wear holy robes to become holy?

I do not believe any of the above questions will answer our problem. Jesus said very clearly that we need to seek "His kingdom and His righteousness." I believe the answer is right there. He said we cannot enter the kingdom if we depend on our righteousness that we earn by doing good works. If it were so, the Scripture would contradict itself because the Bible says our righteousness is like filthy rags before God (Isaiah 64:6).

The only righteousness that exceeds the righteousness of the Pharisees is the righteousness of God Himself! How do we receive it? God bestows His righteousness freely upon everyone who believes in the Lord Christ Jesus. We cannot enter the kingdom based on our works, the way we look, or by the good long prayers we pray.

The Bible says that no one is justified by the works of the law. And if anyone still depends on the works of the law he is under a curse (Galatians 3:10; Romans 3:20 & 28; Philippians 3:9).

"But now the righteousness of God apart from the law is revealed, being witnessed by the Law and the Prophets, even the righteousness of God, through faith in Jesus Christ, to all and on all who believe. For there is no difference" (Romans 3:21-22).

It is very difficult to accept the fact that God will declare a sinner righteous because He believes in Christ. Our natural mind will not accept that and we tend to add stuff to it to feel better about ourselves. It is our fallen human nature to try to look good before others and do good things to feel better and be accepted by other people. The whole religious system of the world is geared toward one thing: encouraging people to do good things so they can escape the wrath of God or the gods they believe in.

The Bible is the only book that teaches righteousness by faith. It teaches that God accepts a person not based on their *work* but on their *faith* and faith alone. So it is difficult for people to believe and receive the free gift of God.

They are ignorant of the fact that they have already been accepted by God, and all they need to do is believe it (Romans 5:8,10). Jesus came to declare the acceptable year of the Lord. What does that mean? He came to declare that God is not angry at people and that He accepts them and loves them for who they are, not based on their works.

This is because all of humanity, except Adam, became sinful not by their choice. As the Bible says, because of one man's disobedience everyone became a sinner and so because of the obedience of one man God declared everyone righteous (Romans 5:18).

So if you want to enter the kingdom, do not boast of your personal achievements or performance, but receive the free gift and walk in it.

> "For by grace you have been saved through faith, and that not of yourselves; *it is* the gift of God, not of works, lest anyone should boast" (Ephesians 2:8).

Jesus did the work for us and paid the price for our freedom, and what a liberty that God has provided for us! Does that mean we do not need to do anything good since we are freely declared righteous? God forbid. Good works are a foundational teaching of the Bible. The heart and reason behind it is what matters now. We do not do any good works to be accepted by God; we do good works because we are righteous and accepted by God. Righteous people do righteous works. Righteous works do not make an unrighteous person righteous at any cost. In the Pauline epistles, it is interesting to see how much Paul encourages the leaders and believers to be involved in good works (See Romans 2:10; Romans 13:3; Ephesians 2:10; 1 Timothy 2:10, and many others).

2) Matthew 7:21:

> "Not everyone who says to Me, 'Lord, Lord,' shall enter the kingdom of heaven, but he who does the will of My Father in heaven."

Once you accept Christ and are born again, you have a special assignment from God, which is the will of God or the call of God for your life. There are two dimensions to the will of God.

1. One is to obey the Word of God, which is the revealed will of God. This is general for all believers and there is no distinction. We are all commanded to obey the Word regardless of our circumstances or status. God has a will for each area of your life. The Word teaches us about family life, finances, raising children, relationships. God has written what to do and what not to do about everything that pertains to our life in His Word. If we reject the Word, we are rejecting God because the Word is God. When you receive the Word and respect it as God's Word, then God will reveal the next dimension of His will.

2. The second is the specific will of God. We are all different members of the same body. Each member in our body has a specific function. Our legs cannot do what our eyes can do and the eyes cannot do what the ears can do. It is the same in the body of Christ. We are all different members of the same body with different functions. God created each individual uniquely and with a unique calling and gifts.

It is the responsibility of each person to find out his or her specific purpose and fulfill it. We do not see God using two people the same way in the Bible. God does not call all of us the same way.

3) Matthew 18:2-3:

> "Then Jesus called a little child to Him, set him in the midst of them, and said, "Assuredly, I say to you, unless you are converted and become as little children, you will by no means enter the kingdom of heaven."

I wondered many times why Jesus said we have to be like children to enter the kingdom of heaven. Then God gave me three precious children and I learned the nature of children from them. We can learn great wisdom from children. I believe our sinful nature gets more rotten the longer we live on this earth. Before they reach the age to know sin or accountability, there is a form of innocence and godliness in most children.

There are a few qualities that I found in children that will help us to understand the reason Jesus said that. There is a difference between childlike and childishness. God does not want us to be childish but childlike. I want to mention some of those qualities. When Jesus talked about children, He meant children from the ages of three to eight.

Innocence: Children are not judgmental of people.

Imitation: They will try to imitate whatever their parents, siblings, or their friends do.

Forget offenses easily: If we offend a child or discipline them it does not stay in their mind for too long. They do not keep today's offenses for tomorrow. I wish I were like that.

Eager to learn new things: They are inquisitive. They are always open to learn new things and go to new places.

Easily Offended: Though they forget offenses easily, they will get offended easily.

Content: They can spend hours with you and never get tired of you.

Quick to make new friends: Children have a special discernment to know people and with those they discern to be safe they will make friends easily.

Quick to believe: It does not take much to make a child believe in something. If I tell my three-year-old there is an elephant behind the couch, she will quickly believe it.

No concept of worry: Children do not worry about tomorrow, neither are they anxious about their present circumstances.

They are always joyful: Children are always joyful and it takes an adult to make them stop being joyful.

Pure and undefiled: Children speak from their heart. They don't have any concept of sin or wrongdoing.

Forget things easily: We need to keep reminding a child the same things again and again. The Bible says we need to exhort each other daily (Hebrews 3:13) to be in faith and to walk in love.

Easily excited and happy: It does not take much to make a child happy.

Need constant training: A child needs to be taught how to live. For some reason human beings are not born with the ability to survive as other animals are. If a child does not have a parent or someone to take care of them, they will die.

Similarly, when we come into the kingdom of God we need to be taught about this new way of living. We come in like a little child and need to learn the ways of God in order to prosper. A new believer needs to be taught about everything when he or she comes into the kingdom of God.

They have no fear: Children do not have a concept of fear as adults do. Their fear is superficial and when an adult tells them to do something they believe it and do it.

The Bible says God has not given us a spirit of fear, but of power, love, and a sound mind (2 Timothy 1:7). I have heard that the Bible says, "Do not fear" 365 times, one for each day of the year. If there is one thing that hinders us from living the life God called us to live, it is the spirit of fear.

They will ask for anything: One thing children are famous for is asking questions about everything. They will ask for a million dollars, though they may not know what it means to have a million dollars.

We are commanded to ask for anything we need in our lives. God said in Jeremiah to call upon Him and He will answer and show us great and mighty things we do not know (Jeremiah 33:3) Jesus said ask and we shall receive (Matthew 7:7).

They are energetic: Children are full of energy and vitality.

***

Take some time and fill in the following points. Have a group discussion about each one.

Imagination:

_____

_____

_____

Full of love:

_____

_____

_____

Free:

_____

_____

_____

Tell the truth:

_____

_____

_____

They do not judge others based on looks:

_____

_____

_____

They will do anything you ask them to do:

_____

_____

_____

They are always pretending to be somebody great:

_____

_____

_____

They are fun to be with:

_____

_____

_____

Very creative:

_____

_____

_____

They have no concept of sin:

_____

_____

_____

They are willing to share with those they love:

_____

_____

_____

They need to be trained and taught constantly about everything in life:

_____

_____

_____

They need adult supervision:

_____

_____

_____

4) Mark 10:15:

> "Assuredly, I say to you, whoever does not receive the kingdom of God as a little child will by no means enter it."

When we receive other people into the kingdom, we have to receive them as we receive a little child. Children are wonderful but they will mess things up and come in with dirty clothes. We need to have the patience to help people clean up as we would help little children.

5) John 3:5:

> "Jesus answered, "Most assuredly, I say to you, unless one is born of water and the Spirit, he cannot enter the kingdom of God."

Jesus said unless we are born of water (the Word) and the Spirit (the Holy Spirit), we will not enter the kingdom. What does this mean? Man is a three-part being. When you receive Christ, your spirit is born again, and that is when you see the kingdom in your spirit. But you have a soul and a body that need to be born again too.

How do our soul and body become born again?

Our soul, which is made of our mind, intellect, will, and memory, needs to be renewed by the Word on a daily basis. Until our thinking process is completely renewed and we reach a place where we naturally think according to the Word of God, we will keep going through trials. This is a process that takes time and is not easily accomplished. The Bible calls it renewing our mind (Romans 12:2).

The moment we are born again in the spirit, God starts the process for our soul and body to become born again too. Most people don't complete this process, in the same way that the majority of the Israelites who came out of Egypt did not inherit the Promised Land, but perished in the wilderness. They were saved, but could not bring their soul and body under subjection to the will and plan of God. They saw the Promised Land (destiny) in their spirit, but could not enter. It is easy to be born again in our spirit—all we have to do is believe and confess that Jesus Christ is Lord. But for our soul and body to be born again we have to die many deaths. We need to be crucified daily like the Bible says (see Romans 6:6; Galatians 2:20; 5:24; 6:14).

Our Promised Land is the dimension of the kingdom of God we enter and experience here on earth. Our body also needs to come under the total submission and leading of the Holy Spirit because our body is the temple of the Holy Spirit (1 Corinthians 3:16; 6:19). We have so many believers in our churches who have been born again in the spirit, but their souls and bodies are still in captivity to the kingdom of darkness. I am sorry to say that they are not living in God's kingdom. It is not their fault; they were not taught correctly. That is why God allowed me to prepare this teaching.

6) Acts 14:21-22:

> "And when they had preached the gospel to that city and made many disciples, they returned to Lystra, Iconium, and Antioch, strengthening the souls of the disciples, exhorting *them* to continue in the faith, and *saying,* "We must through many tribulations enter the kingdom of God."

There is suffering that we go through as part of our transformation from a natural way of thinking to the kingdom way of thinking. There are three areas from which we can expect suffering and tribulation.

Mental Agony and Stress: When we come into the kingdom we come in with a different mindset. As we try to pull those strongholds down and renew our mind we will go through pain because it is not an easy task. We are programmed to function in a certain way; to speak, think, and act and change those into a new system will take time, practice, and much patience.

Attack from Demonic Forces: When you accept Christ and become a child of God you will become a target of the enemy. The enemy will try to harass, deceive, and distract you in an effort to pull you back into the old fold. But know that you are victorious in Christ Jesus. I can guarantee that since it is a battle there will be casualties and days you are disappointed and want to quit. Please know that this is normal. You need to persist in believing and speaking.

Attack from family, fellow believers, and unbelievers: People who will not understand you will try to oppose you and give you much pain. Always know that people are not your enemy because we do not fight against flesh and blood but against spiritual forces. God will use everything you go through for your good in the end. As a preacher once said, "Everything in your life is either God sent or God used." As long as we live on this earth we will have tribulation. But Jesus said to be of good cheer, because He has overcome the world (John 16:33).

147

2 Peter 1:10-11:

"Therefore, brethren, be even more diligent to make your call and election sure, for if you do these things you will never stumble; for so an entrance will be supplied to you abundantly into the everlasting kingdom of our Lord and Savior Jesus Christ."

Make Your Calling Sure

Out of all the people who are alive on the earth today, very few know why they exist. More than 90 percent of the world's population does not know their life's purpose. This includes people who call themselves Christians. That is scary and dangerous at the same time. That means 90 percent of the people who come to church on a Sunday morning do not know their purpose. If you ask Christians the purpose of their life, some will say "to glorify God" or "to worship God." These answers do not hearken to their individual purpose for living. Although we glorify God by fulfilling our purpose, we must find it to do that and really glorify God.

God made our purpose so simple, a child can find and understand it. I did not understand my purpose for a long time because I was blinded by the religious spirit. Though it was the motto of our ministry, to help others discover and fulfill their purpose, for some reason it seemed very complicated until one day the Lord opened my eyes. Then I understood that every human being on this earth has the same purpose. Genesis 1:26 is our purpose statement given to us by our Creator.

It's like the purpose of a car. Every car is made for the same purpose, which is transportation. But, there are different types and sizes of cars, like racecars, taxis, etc. Though every human has the same purpose we are all created differently, in different shapes and sizes, and with different callings and gifts to fulfill that purpose.

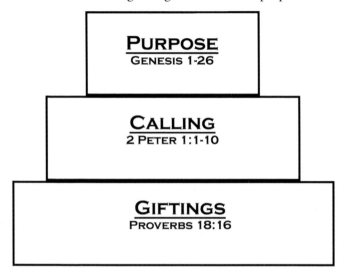

We were created to have dominion on earth. Dominion means to subdue and rule. Every person is created to subdue and rule at least one aspect of life. It could be anything; there are millions and millions of aspects of life. To fulfill that purpose, God calls each one of us to do a specific task. To fulfill that calling He anoints us with different gifts. Each of our callings is different. David was called to be a king; Paul was called to be an apostle. There are different types of gifts; natural gifts, developed gifts, motivational gifts, spiritual gifts, and ministry gifts.

2 Peter 1:10-11 instructs us to make our calling and election sure first, so that we may gain an entrance into the everlasting kingdom of our Father. It says if we do that, we will never stumble. God revealed His calling to me when I was eighteen years old. Since then, I have never had to worry about having

food, clothing, or lodging. It has been nearly 40 years, and God has been faithful. Once you understand the purpose of mankind, the next step is to discover your calling.

Discovering Your Calling Is Important for the Following Reasons:

Your Provision Is Connected to Your Calling

Your financial blessing is attached to your calling. The reason for poverty on earth is because people do not know their purpose and calling. Many nations think population is the problem, and the reason for poverty. Population is not the problem. Productivity is the problem. People not knowing their purpose is the real problem. Many developed nations do not have enough people to do the work, so they allow people from other nations to immigrate to their countries.

Your Provision Is in the Place of Your Calling

Your calling is also connected to a place. Once you discover your calling, you need to know where you are supposed to fulfill it. Depending on the season of your life and your purpose, you might be required to move to a new location. It is the geographic will of God. Many miss God because they are hesitant to move when they should. Each person has a specific place and nation where they are supposed to fulfill their purpose.

Calling Gives You Freedom

We all like having the freedom to do what is really important to us. We like to see places and help other people. When you are doing what you were created to do, it frees you up from being a slave to a system or being tied to a mundane schedule.

Once you discover your calling, you will be able to create your own schedule.

Calling Gives You Fulfillment

Nothing else gives you more satisfaction and fulfillment than doing what you were created to do. Many people are not satisfied and feel unfulfilled, so they try to find fulfillment in the wrong places. Some feel they need a hobby to make them happy.

Calling Gives You Significance

I hope you remember the six basic needs I mentioned earlier that every human is looking to meet. One of them is the need to feel significant. The solution to feeling insignificant is to discover your calling and gifts. When you have a calling and your calling is different from everyone else's, it naturally makes you feel significant. People in the world do all kinds of crazy things to be appreciated and noticed by others. They are trying to fill that need for significance.

Calling Gives You Direction and Focus

Many people do many things, but they do not do anything well because they do not have any focus. Every journey has a destination. Your life has a destiny, which is your destination. When you know what you are supposed to do, you can really focus on it. It also gives you direction about where to go with your life.

Calling Gives You Boundaries

Everything God created has a boundary. Jesus said the path to life is narrow and difficult (Matthew 7:14). It means that living dedicated to your purpose is not easy. Your calling keeps you undistracted and on a narrow path.

Purpose Will Stop Much of the Evil That Is Going On in the Nations

Where there is poverty and lack of purpose, there is an increased rate of crime and all sorts of evil. When people do not know their purpose, they have nothing to do with their time. As the old adage goes, "Idle hands are the devil's workshop." When people discover their purpose, they will be busy working to fulfill it and have no time for anything else. The reason for poverty, drug abuse, rape, divorce, theft, gangs, terrorism, corruption, and all the evil in the world stems from people not knowing their purpose. When people discover their purpose, most of these social problems will disappear from our society and inner cities.

How Do We Discover Our Calling and Gifts?

God sent His Holy Spirit to help us with everything we need. Most people need help discovering their purpose, calling, and gifts. The Holy Spirit is the only person who knows what is in the heart of God concerning you and me. If you believe that you have received the Holy Spirit and still have no sense of purpose, I would double check to see if you received the real Holy Spirit. There are many kinds of spirits on this earth.

"But as it is written:

"'Eye has not seen, nor ear heard, nor have entered into the heart of man the things which God has prepared for those who love Him.' But God has revealed *them* to us through His Spirit. For the Spirit searches all things, yes, the deep things of God. For what man knows the things of a man except the spirit of the man which is in him? Even so no one knows the things of God except the Spirit of God. Now we have received, not the spirit of the world, but the Spirit who is from God, that we might know the things that have been freely given to us by God" (1 Corinthians 2:9-12).

The above passage says that if you love God, He has prepared something very special for you that no one else knows about. If you do not know your calling, there are three basic questions to ask yourself: Do you love God more than anything else on this earth? Did you receive the Holy Spirit? Do you pray? It is the responsibility of the Holy Spirit to show us what God has prepared for us.

If you ask most Christians if they love God, they will say yes. But if you study their lives, you will find that they have no time for God. People make time for what they love, no matter how busy they are. You long to spend time with the one you love the most. If you would like to know more about purpose and how to discover it, please read *The Three Most Important Decisions of Your Life*.

Vision Versus Ambition

Another word for calling is vision. There are many people walking around who think they have a vision from God. I want you to clearly understand the difference between a God-given calling (vision) and selfish ambition. A vision from God will always be centered on other people. It will be for the uplifting or benefit of others. Selfish ambition is always self-centered; it's all about what you want and can have.

One day I was riding in a rickshaw (a three-wheeled taxi) in India with a friend of mine. When it stopped at a light, I looked on the right on the side of the road and saw a little girl playing in the mud. She was only wearing torn underwear. Though this happened more than fifteen years ago, I can still see her in my heart as if it were yesterday. I had seen hundreds of children like that before, but when I saw that little girl I began to cry. I looked at my friend and he was crying too. I heard a voice in my spirit, say, "You need to do something about this."

The only thing I knew at that time that I could do for such children was to start an orphanage, so I prayed and decided to do that. We ran that children's home for fourteen years, and many poor and orphaned children went through our program. Some of them are in ministry today. The reason I am sharing this story is to give you an example of a vision that is from God.

Why are many of our prayers not getting answered? God only answers prayers that are in line with His kingdom purpose for us. That is why His Word tells us,

> "Now this is the confidence that we have in Him, that
> if we ask anything according to His will, He hears us"
> (1 John 5:14).

The "dream big" philosophy is not of God's kingdom. God never appeared to anybody and told them to dream the biggest dream. Instead, He always had detailed instructions for each person to do something specific. The "dream big" philosophy was birthed from humanism, which unfortunately also crept into the church.

Below are the seven qualities of a God-given vision or calling:

1. It is always for the benefit of others

The vision God gives you will be a blessing to someone else or to a particular group of people. God saw a problem that needs to be solved and created you and put the vision in your heart to solve it. As you solve that problem, you will also be blessed in turn. If you look at any great achievement, the main beneficiary of that achievement is the general public.

2. It is impossible to accomplish by yourself

A God-given vision always requires the help of others. It will take a team to accomplish any purpose in the kingdom. If you can accomplish the vision by yourself, then it is not of God.

3. Your current circumstances will be contradictory to the vision God gives you

When God puts a vision in your heart, your circumstances will not seem to support it. It will look like there is no way it could ever happen. God might put a vision in your heart to be a king, but you might be out in the wilderness taking care of someone else's sheep. You might be called to own a business, but right now you are working as a salesperson at someone else's business.

4. You will have to overcome enormous obstacles to achieve that vision

When God puts His vision in our hearts, He allows us to go through trials and face obstacles. This is to build character and faith in us so that when we are actually fulfilling the vision, we will not fall prey to various temptations.

5. You will not have the resources to fulfill your vision

God knows you do not have the resources to fulfill the vision He puts in your heart. He wants you to depend on kingdom resources and kingdom economy. How did Jesus feed the five thousand without spending any money? He did not run home to ask His mother for help or take an offering from the crowd. He knew how to tap into supernatural resources. We need to learn the same.

6. It will look impossible in the natural

When God promised Abraham and Sarah a son, it looked totally impossible. When the angel Gabriel told the Virgin Mary that she was going to be pregnant and give birth to a son, there was no way it was possible in the natural. So, if your vision seems impossible, welcome to the company of radicals.

7. You will have to go through the death of your vision

When God gives you a vision, you will be all excited and dancing for a while. Then you will go through a season in your life in which that vision will seem totally dead. You will try everything you can to make it happen; but the more you try, the more you will end up disappointed. You will need to learn to leave it alone and surrender your vision to God, and He will bring it to pass in His own time and ways.

Prayer

Dear heavenly Father, thank You so much for giving me Your kingdom and creating me as a king on this earth. Open my eyes to see and receive the mysteries of Your kingdom. Please make me part of what You are doing on this earth right now. I dedicate my life and everything I have to establishing Your kingdom for Your purpose, to see Your will done on earth as it is in heaven. In Jesus Christ's holy name I pray. Amen.

I believe this book has been a blessing to you. Please use it for Bible study groups. We invite you to email us with any questions you may have from this book. Please feel free to share it with others. This is only an introduction to the subject of the kingdom of God. I could only mention here a fraction of the revelation God gave me about His kingdom. I strongly encourage you to get volumes 2, 3, 4, 5 and 6 of the Kingdom Awareness Series: *The Power and Authority of the Church: Equipping the Saints to Administer God's Kingdom on Earth* (Volume 2), *Releasing Kings and Queens to Their Original Intent* (Volume 3), *Kingdom Secrets to Restoring Nations Back to God* (Volume 4), *Kingdom Family* (Volume 5), *Kingdom Economy* (Volume 6), and *Kingdom Government* (Volume 7).

To order more copies of this study guide and other resources, please contact:

Maximum Impact Ministries,
P.O. Box 631460
Littleton, CO 80163-1460

Phone: (720) 420 9873
Email: mim@maximpact.org
www.maximpact.org

More Books by Abraham John

Books

Rediscovering the Lost Kingdom $10.00 (Volume 1)

The Power and Authority of the Church $15.00 (Volume 2)

Releasing Kings and Queens to their Original Intent $15.00 (Volume 3)

Kingdom Secrets to Restoring Nations Back to God $20.00 (Volume 4)

Kingdom Mandate (for any donation)

Kingdom Family $15.00 (Volume 5)

Kingdom Economy $15.00 (Volume 6)

Kingdom Government $15.00 (Volume 7)

7 Dimensions and Operations of the Kingdom of God $10.00

The Three Most Important Decisions of Your Life $15.00

Keys to Passing Your Spiritual Tests $15.00

Recognizing God's Timing For Your Life $12.00

Overcoming the Spirit of Poverty $10.00

Seven Kinds of Believers $10.00

7 Dimensions of God's Glory $5.00

7 Dimensions of God's Grace $10.00

7 Kinds of Faith $7.00

Audio CDs

Kingdom Secrets to Restoring Nations Back to God $10.00

Kingdom Economy $10.00

To place an order:

Maximum Impact Ministries
P.O. Box 631460
Littleton, CO 80163-1460

Phone: (720) 420 9873
Email: mim@maximpact.org
www.maximpact.org